Why People Are Raving about
Driving Profits and Making Bank

"Wow. This is the most thorough book on rideshare driving I can possibly imagine. It's like the encyclopedia for anyone who wants to become a solopreneur by driving for Uber, Lyft, or any other rideshare company. From tips on how to earn more money as a driver to safety issues and business advice, this book will have you on your drive to easy street in no time."

— Tyler R. Tichelaar, Ph.D., Solopreneur of Superior Book Productions and Award-Winning author of *Narrow Lives*

"While this book focuses on rideshare driving for Uber and Lyft, the lessons are applicable to all small business owners just starting out. I remember how hard it was for me when I first started my business many years ago. I wish I'd had a resource like this book to help walk me through things way back when."

— Jeff Bow, Master Certified Coach, Speaker and Author of *Stop Thinking, Start Believing: How to Break Through Fear and Ignite Your Brilliance*

"Timely and practical, Wong provides an excellent roadmap to the ridesharing business. Anyone who has ever thought of moonlighting or pursuing rideshare driving for Uber, Lyft or other services need to read this book."

— Natalie Kawai, Author of
Conversations With Mother Goddess

"Do you want to learn practical ways to earn money, be more effective, develop a solid business mindset, and grow your business? While initially teaching the popular rideshare (Uber) business model, this book goes beyond and shows you how to tap into and leverage additional business opportunities while helping you develop solid business basics."

— Susan Friedmann, CSP, International Bestselling Author of
Riches in Niches: How to Make it BIG in a small Market

"I thought I was going to read about how to make money driving for Uber. What I got was a lot more. Jonathan shares practical advice for running any type of small business."

— Angie Engstrom, Transition Coach, Professional Keynote Speaker, and Author of *Getting Yourself Unstuck.*

"This is such a great and timely book. So many people out there are working in the sharing and on-demand gig economies, but they don't know what their rights are or responsibilities are as independent contractors and small business owners. Small business consultant Jonathan Wong pulls back the curtain and provides great information that is helpful to all 1099 workers."

— Laurie Bethell Bratt, Professional Holistic Health Coach, Certified Transformational Breath Facilitator, Author of *Bear Witness: Striving to Live Each Moment Like It Is Your Last*

"Jonathan Wong gives a very exhaustive review of the popular ridesharing industry. Technically well-written. If you are interested in this industry, this is the book for you."

— T. Paul Neustrom, Best Seller Publishing

"This book is a true compendium of advice and resources that anyone who is starting out in the ridesharing business really needs to read. The point, of course, is that it *is* a business and you need to treat it that way if you're going to make any money at it. Mr. Wong makes it very clear that this isn't a bag of magic beans leading to instant riches: If you treat it as a hobby that pays, you could end up making sub-minimum wage if not actually running in the red. More experienced rideshare drivers will also find the book useful for the ideas offered to help you maximize your ride income and for the numerous ways suggested to provide complementary income streams to turn a modest second income into a real sustainable business. The book is easy reading, yet very thorough. You can get through it easily enough in a couple of hours, but, like any good reference book, the whole idea isn't to memorize it. This is one that you'll be coming back to again and again when you want to remind yourself of one of the great insights you read earlier."

— Douglas Brown, Ph.D., Managing Member, Decision Integration LLC, a business consultancy

"Jonathan Wong provides many great small business lessons applicable to all small business owners. This is more than just an Uber book. Anyone looking to start a small business can benefit from the lessons presented here."

— Kapono R. Kobylanski, MBA, Author of *Waking Up: With No Excuses*

"This book is so helpful for anyone out there trying to make a living as an Uber driver or elsewhere in the on-demand and sharing economy. Most folks are not trained as business people but are suddenly thrust into the world of independent contractors and don't know what they are doing. Wong's *Driving Profits* provides a detailed roadmap on what needs to be done and how to do it as an independent contractor driver partner. Highest recommendation."

— Heather Howell, Author of
Dream It, See It, Believe It

"This is the book that all rideshare drivers need. When starting out driving for Uber and Lyft, the training as an independent contractor status is minimal to non-existent. Wong provides excellent information and resources on how to get your small business up and running and provides great information on how to leverage your rideshare business. Anyone with or without business training will benefit from his insights and how to develop a better business mind."

— Phyliss Francis-Wigfall, Author of
Breaking Through Your Glass Ceiling

DRIVING
PROFITS
AND
MAKING
BANK

HOW TO MAKE MONEY
RIDESHARING AND
GROW YOUR BUSINESS

JONATHAN WONG, MBA, M.ED, MPA

AVIVA
PUBLISHING
New York

Driving Profits and Making Bank: How to Make Money Ridesharing and Grow Your Business

Copyright © 2017 by Jonathan Wong

Address all inquiries to:
Jonathan Wong
P.O. Box 23259
Honolulu, HI 96823
(213) 262-9570
www.drivingprofitsandmakingbank.com

ISBN: 978-1-9443350-0-7
Library of Congress Control Number: 2016958256

Editor: Tyler Tichelaar, Superior Book Productions
Cover and Interior Design: Nicole Gabriel, AngelDog Productions

Published by:
Aviva Publishing
Lake Placid, NY
(518) 523-1320
www.avivapubs.com

Every attempt has been made to source properly all quotes.

Printed in the USA
First Edition

For additional copies visit:

www.drivingprofitsandmakingbank.com

DISCLAIMER

The material provided in this book is for informational purposes only and not for the purpose of providing business or financial advice. You should contact your business, legal, or financial advisor to obtain advice with respect to any particular issue or problem for your specific situation. Use of this book and the materials contained within do not create an advisor-client relationship between Jonathan Wong, The Pono Way, LLC and the reader. The opinions expressed herein are the opinions of the individual author. Any business, legal, or financial decisions you make are yours and yours alone, and you bear the ultimate responsibility for any results that may occur. There are many market conditions and government regulations that affect your chance of success with any decisions you make, and neither Jonathan Wong nor The Pono Way, LLC is liable for any losses or perceived losses you may incur. You are advised to work with qualified business, financial, and legal consultants prior to making any firm decisions.

DEDICATION

To my instructors at the University of Hawai'i Shidler College of Business (Jack Suyderhoud, David Bess, Kiyohiko Ito, David Bangert, Linda Harris [RIP], James Richardson, Rob Robinson, Stephen Vargo, Reg Worthley, Mary Woollen), and my classmates in the Shidler MBA Class of 2007 (Lyle, Shane, Pam, Mana, Ola, Jen, Chris, Mel, Sooz) for the thorough grounding in business that allowed me to grow my business and write this book with confidence.

To my fellow drivers in Rideshare808. Thank you for your camaraderie, for the laughs all day, every day, and for venting war stories about life on the road.

To my parents, Allen and Charlotte, and my brother, Mike, and sister-in-law, Maureen, for supporting me and loving me through it all.

And finally, to my love, Liane. Thank you for staying by me through good times and lean times and for giving me the freedom to pursue my dreams and build my business and our future together. I love you.

ACKNOWLEDGMENTS

A big mahalo (thank you) to the following individuals without whom this book would not have been possible.

To Patrick Snow, the greatest book publishing and marketing coach on the planet. Patrick taught me and helped me realize my dreams of becoming a published author.

To Nicole Gabriel for the most beautiful book covers on the planet.

To Tyler Tichelaar who makes me sound even more sophisticated and intelligent.

To Brodi Goshi, Jodi Uehara, John Noland, and Justine Gronwald who helped support and promote my rideshare ventures at the outset.

CONTENTS

PREFACE

"You give a poor man a fish and you feed him for a day. You teach him to fish and you give him an occupation that will feed him for a lifetime."

— Anne Isabella Thackeray Ritchie

As a former college instructor, a life coach, and a business consultant, one of my driving purposes in life is to help people grow the lives they wish and deserve to live. In our modern society, we all have the need to make money. We need it to pay for food, shelter, clothing, education, and to provide opportunities to our children, such as music or dance lessons and playing sports. We need money to realize our dreams, make a down payment on a house, go on our dream trip across the globe, have our dream wedding, or buy that new car. Sometimes, we need more than we have, so we need more to get out of debt. Everyone needs money.

DRIVING PROFITS AND MAKING BANK

The recent rise of sharing and on-demand economies present us with many unique opportunities:

- We can earn extra money to meet our bills and dig ourselves out of debt.

- We can save money to fund our long-term goals and dreams like buying a home, sending our kids to college, or to go on our dream trips.

- We can even become our own bosses and break out of the 9-5 cycle.

I'm a firm believer in entrepreneurship as the key to building our dreams. In our world of downsizing, failed businesses, or layoffs, you can't rely on your job always to be there for you. Everyone needs a backup plan—a "Plan B." I believe business skills are one of the key life skills you need to learn if you truly want to get ahead in life. Unfortunately, not everyone can afford an expensive business degree. I was fortunate in my life to have had the opportunity to study business and earn a Master of Business Administration. One of my life's passions is to share my business knowledge with others so they too can start and own their own businesses, whether they are solopreneurs working for themselves, employ a small team of assistants in a true small business, or they band together with a group of friends to found the next major life-changing startup.

PREFACE

The goal of this book is threefold: 1) To teach you the basics of the ridesharing business and how it works, 2) To teach you about ways you can leverage ridesharing to expand into other business opportunities, and 3) To teach you the basic business management skills you need to stay out of financial or legal trouble. It is my hope that you'll be able to use the knowledge and skills I cover in this book either to run your own ridesharing business successfully or to pursue any other dreams or passions you have so you can make your living on your own terms as an entrepreneur.

I spent two years of my life and approximately $30,000.00 to earn my graduate level business degree. In the confines of this short book, I will share with you what I learned in business school and how to apply it to the world of ridesharing. You can use this information to start your own part-time or full-time career as a rideshare driver or to start and build on other opportunities.

I want to be your coach, your mentor, and your accountability partner in fulfilling your business and entrepreneurial dreams! Starting a business is not easy to do or something to taken lightly. Much like it took Edison a thousand tries before he invented the lightbulb, launching and running a successful business takes a lot of trial and error and savvy know-how. Most businesses ultimately fail. If you're looking to get into the rideshare business and truly grow and expand it to make a comfortable living for yourself, it'll take lots of support from seasoned drivers and business professionals who know about not only rideshare but just good business in general. I invite you to include me in your support network as you begin your small business journey. I will share with you all the tools, tips, and techniques I used to launch not only my own successful rideshare business, but my other business ventures that have allowed me to create the life I want on my terms, free from the demands of being locked into a 9-5 job, and free to take on and choose the opportunities and projects I wish to pursue.

So are you ready to set yourself up for America's easiest and most flexible money-making opportunity? Are you ready to become your own boss, set your own hours, and take home cash every single day? Are you ready to learn good, basic, and sound business skills that will lay the foundation for this and any other business venture you'll ever set your heart on? If so, let's get started!

To your business and life success!

With aloha, your friend,

Jonathan K Wong

Jonathan Wong, MBA, M.Ed., MPA
Honolulu, Hawaii

FOREWORD

BY PATRICK SNOW

When I began my career as a professional speaker, author, and coach, I honestly didn't really know that much about business on the theoretical and practical sides. I had to learn things the hard way through much trial and error, and at first, I made a lot of mistakes. Fortunately, through meeting and mentoring under great business minds, I eventually honed my craft as a business person, and over the years, I took their teachings to heart. As a result, I've been able to forge a successful speaking, writing, and coaching career.

Through all my years as a successful business owner and as someone who has studied under the best business minds on the planet, I have discovered that successful people always study other successful people to achieve their successes. They study them. They take and apply their teachings and best practices, and they integrate those into their own practices and businesses. Ultimately, if you want to be a success, you need to learn, copy, and apply from successful people.

In this powerful book by my great friend Jonathan Wong, you will learn solid business skills and develop an entrepreneurial and business mindset as it relates to the world of rideshare driving. *Driving Profits and Making Bank* is the most comprehensive walk through of the rideshare business for prospective and current Uber and Lyft drivers. It also provides a comprehensive walk through of everything that all small-business owners need or need to think about in starting their own businesses. The solid business tips and skills Jonathan shares are exactly what I wish someone had shared with me when I started my business more than twenty-five years ago.

When you follow the formulas and strategies in this book, you will discover that your mind will expand and grow in ways you never thought of before. You will start to see the world through the eyes of an entrepreneur and start to see possibilities and opportunities where you did not previously. You will develop business savvy and build confidence to test new waters and provide for yourself and your family in ways you never thought of before.

Through this book, you will learn that the drive to success must come from within you, but it takes a strong support system to help you maintain your drive and accomplish your goals. Let Jonathan be a driving force to assist you to be the person you were meant to be. As a result, you will experience, realize, and achieve your destiny.

So...get ready for an amazing ride as you embark on your entrepreneurial career as a rideshare driver and beyond in *Driving Profits and Making Bank*.

Patrick Snow

Patrick Snow

Publishing Coach and International Best-Selling Author of *Creating Your Own Destiny, The Affluent Entrepreneur, Boy Entrepreneur,* and *Providing Massive Value*
www.PatrickSnow.com
www.ThePublishingDoctor.com

PART I
RIDESHARE BASICS

CHAPTER 1

WHAT IS RIDESHARING?

"If you don't drive your business,
you will be driven out of business."

— B.C. Forbes

Ridesharing Defined

Ridesharing has changed the way we commute from place to place, whether we are traveling on vacation or for business, getting to and from work or school, or simply heading to the store to get a carton of milk. For many, ridesharing has changed the way they make a living. Whether they wanted to break out of the 9-5 routine, earn extra money to save for a trip, get out of debt, or just needed another job with flexible hours simply to scrape by, ridesharing has provided them with extra income. Ridesharing has changed our world. For all of its conveniences and penetration into the market, though, many people are still not familiar with it. They may have heard of Uber or Lyft, but that is the extent of it. They know "It's like a cab, but not."

So to start off, here's a simple definition of ridesharing:

"A smartphone app facilitated service matching everyday drivers who are able to give a ride to everyday passengers in need of a ride."

In other words, both the driver and passenger need a smartphone with the appropriate app installed to get matched by a Transportation Network Company (TNC) such as Uber or Lyft.

Eligibility Requirements

You may be reading this book because you've always been interested in driving for Uber, Lyft, or similar companies, but you aren't too sure what it's like or where to start. Therefore, we'll start at the beginning. While eligibility requirements vary from city to city or state to state, following are the general requirements. I encourage you to research the Uber or Lyft websites for current information specific to your city.

WHAT IS RIDESHARING?

Generally speaking, to become a driver, both you and your car must meet eligibility requirements.

Driver Eligibility

To drive for Uber, Lyft, or similar companies, you need to meet the following driver eligibility requirements:

- Be twenty-one years of age or older
- Have a valid driver's license
- Have a driving history (three years for Uber, one year for Lyft)
- Have a clean driving record (no DUI, drug, or reckless driving convictions in the past seven years)
- Pass a background check (no violent or sex crime convictions)
- Have a legally registered vehicle
- Possess a personal insurance policy for your car or be listed as a covered driver
- Additional requirements as imposed by your local jurisdiction

DRIVING PROFITS AND MAKING BANK

Car Eligibility

Assuming you meet the driver eligibility requirements, your car must also meet the eligibility requirements. Again, while requirements vary from city to city, following are the general requirements that apply nationwide. Again, check the Uber or Lyft websites for car requirements specific to your city and for the latest information.

Uber has the following minimum requirements for driver cars:

- Four-door sedan, seats five passengers with five seat belts (including driver)

- Year 2001 or newer (some states or cities require 2005 or newer)

- Current registration, in-state plates, safety check, and insurance

- No taxi or commercial markings

- Uber's premium services (XL, SELECT, BLACK, SUV, LUX) have additional requirements

- Your state or local government may also have additional requirements

WHAT IS RIDESHARING?

Lyft has the following minimum requirements for driver cars:

- Four-door sedan, seats five passengers with five seat belts (including driver)

- Year 2004 or later (some states or cities may require later)

- Current registration, in-state plates, safety check, and insurance

- Pass a Lyft safety inspection during a Mentor Session

- Your state or local government may also have additional requirements

Technical Requirements

For both Uber and Lyft, you will need to have a current smart-phone, iPhone4 with OS7 or later, or an Android 4.0 phone or later. The Uber and Lyft apps only support the iOS (iPhone) or Android platforms.

The Apps

To drive and accept ride requests, you must have the Uber or Lyft apps downloaded and installed on your phone.

DRIVING PROFITS AND MAKING BANK

Uber Driver Partner App

As a driver for Uber, you will need the "Uber Driver" app. This is separate from the "Uber" app, which is what you use to request rides.

Lyft App

Lyft's app is a dual purpose app, which has "Driver" and "Rider" sides and functions to it. If you are currently a Lyft rider, you can access the "Driver" side of the app once you become approved to be a driver.

Getting Fares

To get ride requests from passengers as a Driver, you simply need to log in to the Driver app and "Go Online" to make yourself available to receive ride requests. Once you are "Online," Uber or Lyft will start to filter ride requests to you from the nearest ride requester.

You simply "accept" an incoming ride request; then the app takes over using your phone's GPS system to give you turn-by-turn directions to the pickup point.

WHAT IS RIDESHARING?

When you're ready to call it a shift and want to stop taking ride requests (or you need a bathroom break!), simply "Go Offline" and you won't receive ride requests any longer.

It really is that simple!

Summary

In this first chapter, I gave you a brief overview of the requirements you need to meet to become a driver alongside the requirements your car needs to meet. You need a current smartphone (iPhone or Android) with the Uber Driver or Lyft apps installed. You must be twenty-one years of age or older, possess a valid driver's license, have a clean driving record and no criminal history, and carry personal auto insurance. You must have a car no older than fifteen years that seats five passengers or more (including yourself). Requirements vary from city to city so you are encouraged to check the Uber or Lyft websites for the latest, most current information for your specific city. I then gave you a brief rundown of the process of "Going Online" to make yourself eligible to receive rides and how to accept them. Being a driver is a painlessly simple process!

DRIVING PROFITS AND MAKING BANK

Driving Forward

Let's get you ready to get out on the road as a new Driver Partner for Uber or Lyft.

1. Do you meet the driver eligibility requirements?

2. Does your car meet the minimum requirements for your city?

3. Do you have a smartphone that meets the technical requirements?

CHAPTER 2
BENEFITS OF RIDESHARING

"I want to be able to get up every day and be excited about what is happening in my day both professionally and personally and have the means to be able to do the things that bring me joy."

— Kim Harper

The Rearview Mirror

In the last chapter, I gave you a very basic overview of what ridesharing is and explained the facilitation of connecting people who can give rides with people who need rides through a smartphone device and app as offered through a Transportation Network Company (TNC) like Uber or Lyft. In this chapter, I will share the benefits of being a rideshare driver, of which there are many; hence, thousands of people across the country use driving for a rideshare company as a flexible source of income, if not a brand new career outright.

"Easy" Work

As far as tasks go, the work is "easy." Driving is a skill most of us take for granted, especially if we got our driver's licenses as teenagers. You pick people up and drop them off. As far as work goes, it's very simple and basic. You're not standing behind a counter taking orders and bagging people's lunches or drinks. You're not stocking shelves at the supermarket or ringing people up at the checkout line. You're not answering phones all day taking people's complaints or trying to make sales or ask people for donations. You're picking someone up at point A and dropping him or her off at point B. It's relatively mindless work that can be very enjoyable if you like talking with people and don't mind the nuances of traffic.

Freedom of Time

As a rideshare driver, you are an independent contractor, which means you are self-employed. As such, you get to set your own hours. Don't like fighting rush hour traffic? No one is forcing you to. If you want to drive only between 10 a.m. and 2 p.m. to avoid morning and afternoon rush hour, you can. If you only want to drive between 9 p.m. and 12 a.m., you can. If you want to drive between 3 a.m. and 6 a.m. before traffic starts, you can. You have that freedom of time. If you want to stop work so you can go watch your kid's soccer game, baseball game, football game, track meet, or school play, you have that freedom. You don't need to "ask for time off." You have complete freedom of time.

Freedom of the Road

As a driver, you also get to experience the "freedom of the road." Many of us may be used to jobs where we are glued to a desk, a service counter, a sales floor, or a post for eight hours a day. As a rideshare driver, you have the freedom of the road where the scenery changes and each day is a new adventure. Sure, many of the pickup points and drop offs are common, and you'll more than likely be taking many of the same routes day after day, but you'll be outside and not stuck indoors staring at the clock, waiting for quitting time, or inundated by lines or crowds of people waiting to see you. With the freedom of the road, you never know where the lunch hour will take you, and you'll have the freedom to grab lunch wherever you want because you're already out. You won't be needing to bring a lunch from home every day, or walk to one of the same few restaurants near your workplace and rush to get back within sixty minutes.

You Are the Boss

Ultimately, you are your own boss as an independent contractor/driver partner for Uber, Lyft, or whatever rideshare company you partner with. As such, you set your own hours. You work whenever you feel like working—if you feel like working. No one is forcing you to work. You won't be fired if you get sick or don't show up. You won't get written up. You're not locked into an eight-to-five job. You are not required to report at a certain time every day or compelled to stay until a certain time.

You get to work around your schedule and demands. Are you raising kids, so you need to drop them off or pick them up? Want to attend their sporting events, plays, or music recitals? Need to help your elderly parent with weekly chores and shopping? Go right ahead! You're the boss. There are no vacation or leave forms to fill out. Come and go as you please.

Get Paid Weekly or Daily

As a rideshare driver, you have the luxury of continuous cash flow.

BENEFITS OF RIDESHARING

As a standard, Uber and Lyft will pay you what you've earned every week. If you need your money quicker, there are daily pay options where you can get your money the same day or when you reach an earnings threshold, minus a convenience fee. Uber allows you to cash out whenever you want, minus a fee. Lyft requires you to have a balance of $50 before you can choose the daily cash out, and it also charges a convenience fee for this service.

So if you're bank account is nearing zero and you have a bill coming up, or if you need cash for a night out, you can drive and get your money transferred to your bank account right then and there. It really is that simple!

Beats waiting on someone else's payroll schedule, huh?

Perfect Part-Time Gig

Rideshare driving is quite frankly the best part-time gig you'll ever have because of its flexibility and near instantaneous pay. Whether you need extra money to get out of debt, make your rent or mortgage, or to save for a financial goal, you can definitely use driving for Uber or Lyft to meet those goals.

Moonlighting is nothing new here in America. Many of us used to have second and third part-time jobs in retail sales, security, customer service, direct sales, or do things like sign up for the military reserves or National Guard.

Rideshare driving gives you yet another option, but with the convenience of setting your own hours and being able to take home what you earn today. No more trudging off to your second job to start your shift on time (or else) when you're already tired. No more having family or friends shun you when you ask them about "getting in on a great opportunity."

As a part-time gig (or even full-time), rideshare driving is perfect for the following types of folks:

The Full-Time Worker Needing a Part-Time Job

Rideshare driving is great if you already have a full-time job and need a part-time job for extra income to work your way out of debt or make extra cash to save for something big.

Your hours are flexible, so you can drive whenever you want without worrying about rushing between jobs.

Artists, Freelancers, and the Self-Employed

If you're already self-employed as an artist, freelancer, or whatever you may do, you already know what it's like and how to weather the storms of an inconsistent income. No matter what your primary gig is, you'll find that rideshare driving is a great opportunity to earn a steady, base income that can help you get by while you either secure gigs or build up clientele. As a bonus, rideshare driving offers an opportunity to network—sometimes your passengers are in need of what you provide or know other people who might be.

Stay-At-Home Parents or Caregivers

For stay-at-home parents or caregivers, money is always a concern. The selflessness you display in forgoing a career to raise children or care for loved ones comes with a sacrifice— you can't build a career and earn an income. This makes you dependent on a spouse or other family members financially. Families often need as much money as they can get. Alongside running a home-based business, rideshare driving is another valid option for the stay-at-home caregiver, allowing you to generate income while the kids are at school or while Grandma and Grandpa are napping for a few hours. Just turn your app on and you're off accepting rides and earning money.

College Students

Working your way through school is something many of us did.

DRIVING PROFITS AND MAKING BANK

Few are lucky enough to have parents able (or willing) to foot the bill completely. For college students, finding a part-time job that allows time to study is not always easy. Your employer expects you to show up just like regular workers, on time and with your A game, whether you're waiting tables, ringing up groceries, flipping burgers, or checking in hotel guests.

Rideshare driving, if you're fortunate enough to have your own car, allows you to make money while keeping your focus on your studies.

Military Members and Dependents

As a member of the armed forces or a dependent of a service member, you have the privilege of being part of America's fighting force and enjoying many benefits related to housing and cheap goods and services through commissaries and exchanges. That said, the pay may not always be enough to get by financially. As a service member or dependent, rideshare driving provides an opportunity to supplement the pay Uncle Sam gives you. With working and driving at your convenience, you can work during your time off from defending American freedom, or if you're a dependent, while your spouse is on duty.

BENEFITS OF RIDESHARING

Each Day Is a New Adventure

As a rideshare driver, each day will always be a new adventure—you never know who will get into your car or where you will go. You may be off to a theme park or a scenic trail with a group of tourists. You may wind up on the other side of town at some restaurant or club you've never heard of. You may be dropping off a business traveler at a work site in a part of town you didn't know existed. Come lunch time, you never know where you'll be, but you can be sure there'll always be a new foodie adventure awaiting you. Meeting people from all over the world, you'll be exposed to different perspectives and cultures. Rideshare driving can be quite the blessing.

Great Social Job

Rideshare driving is a great social job. You'll get the opportunity to meet all kinds of people from all over the world, be they travelers, new transplants to the area, locals going about daily activities, students, or service members.

No Advertising Required

Perhaps one of the nicest things about rideshare driving is that it truly is a "business in a box." If you've ever run or managed a business before, you'll know how much work it takes to get the word out and make a sale, no matter what your product or service. Rideshare driving is brilliant in the sense that it requires no advertising on your part to get customers. You turn on your phone, log in to your app, and boom! Within ten minutes, you'll get your first ride request and have made your first sale. After that, the app just keeps feeding you ride after ride after ride. It doesn't get easier than that.

No Capital Investment Required

Another benefit to owning an independent rideshare business is that there is no capital investment (unless you don't have a car). Unlike many other businesses, like owning a store, you're not putting up money for an expensive lease or purchasing expensive equipment or inventory. You're simply using the car you already have.

If you drive enough, the money you make will be plenty to pay your car payment. Furthermore, many of your expenses like gas, car insurance, and maintenance become deductible as business expenses for tax purposes.

BENEFITS OF RIDESHARING

Summary

In this chapter, I discussed the benefits of rideshare driving, including the following: easy work using a skill you take for granted, being your own boss and setting your own hours, continuous cash flow with weekly or daily payout options, a part-time or full-time income, socializing with people from all walks of life, and a business opportunity with no advertising costs or capital investment.

Driving Forward

Let's see whether rideshare driving is for you.

1. Would you enjoy driving people around for extra money or as a new career?

2. Do you need extra money to meet financial needs or goals?

3. Do you have extra time you'd otherwise devote to a second job?

4. Do you need an additional income source?

CHAPTER 3

BECOMING A DRIVER

"The journey of a thousand miles begins with a single step."

— Lao Tzu

The Rearview Mirror

In the last chapter, I discussed the many benefits of rideshare driving. In this chapter, I will talk about the process of signing up to drive with Uber or Lyft.

Apply Online

The easiest way to apply is online at both Uber.com and Lyft.com. Your online application will initiate the process.

If you are a new driver applying online, you are welcome to enter the following promotional codes to become eligible for any new driver sign-up benefits happening in your area—promotions vary from city to city.

Uber: Referral Code: 7avf4qscue

Lyft: Referral Code: JONATHAN008938

* Disclosure: These are my personal referral codes. I gain personal benefit if you choose to sign up using these codes. Your choice to use these codes is a personal one, but signing up with a friend's referral code does make you eligible for sign-up bonuses in many markets. Thank you for your consideration.

Have a Car

You will need access to an eligible car (discussed in Chapter 1 and expanded upon in Chapter 4) and the appropriate documentation, which I will cover in the next section.

Submit Documents

As part of the sign-up process, you will need to upload scanned or photographed copies of the following documents:

- Your current, valid driver's license

- Your current, valid vehicle registration certificate

- Your current, valid auto insurance card or documentation confirming you are a covered driver on a valid insurance policy covering the vehicle you will be driving

- Your current safety check sticker or certificate from your local safety check facility if you live in a state that requires one.

Agree to Background Check

As part of the sign-up process, you must agree to a background check. The background check reviews your driving record and criminal history. Processing can take anywhere from a few days to a few weeks.

Additional Company Requirements

Depending on your city, you may be subject to additional requirements by Uber or Lyft. In many cities, Uber requires an Uber-specific safety check at an Uber partner facility.

DRIVING PROFITS AND MAKING BANK

For Lyft, you are required to attend a mentor session with an experienced Lyft driver who will conduct a safety check on your vehicle and administer a road test.

Additional Requirements per Local Laws

Depending on your jurisdiction, your state or local government may have additional requirements before you can start driving. Example requirements may include:

- Business registration
- Registration with airport authorities
- Driver or vehicle permits
- Government emblems or stickers on bumpers
- Vehicle inspections at government-certified facilities
- Additional insurance
- Tests or training
- Medical clearance
- Drug testing
- Fingerprinting
- Driver time limits

The Uber and Lyft websites will detail the requirements for your specific city. Check the sites for current information.

Download the App

Once the application is complete, you'll want to download the Uber Driver app and/or the Lyft app. Both apps are available at the Apple App Store and Google Play Store.

Uber or Lyft Window Decals

Once you are approved to be a driver, both Uber and Lyft will provide you with driver decals for the passenger side of your front window. Per company policy, you must keep the decals on when you are on duty. Local laws may also require you to do so to identify yourself to passengers as a licensed, affiliated driver.

Summary

In this chapter, I discussed the process of signing up to be a driver. The quick and easy process involves filling out an online application, uploading your driver and car documents, consenting to a background check, and downloading the phone apps. Once approved, you will receive driver decals you are required to display on your passenger window while on duty, per company policy and many local laws.

Driving Forward

Let's get you signed up with Uber and/or Lyft so you are ready to hit the road and make some cash!

- Fill out the online applications at Uber.com and/or Lyft. com.

- Scan or take a picture of your driver's license.

- Scan or take a picture of your vehicle registration.

- Scan or take a picture of your auto insurance card.

- Scan or take a picture of your safety inspection.

- Research whether your city has any additional requirements for becoming a rideshare driver. (Uber and Lyft sites will have this information.)

CHAPTER 4

DRIVER PROGRAMS AND CARS

"All animals are equal, but some animals are
more equal than others."

— George Orwell

The Rearview Mirror

In the previous chapter, we looked at the process of signing up to become a rideshare driver with Uber and Lyft. In this chapter, I will discuss the different levels of driver services classes available and vehicle requirements. Your earning potential is affected by the type of car you drive and the service class you're eligible for.

DRIVING PROFITS AND MAKING BANK

Car Age Limits

Car age requirements for Uber and Lyft were detailed in Chapter 1, but in general, cars need to be between ten and fifteen years old or newer, depending on your city. Each city sets its own requirements for vehicle age, so it is best to visit the Uber or Lyft websites to find your specific city and its current requirements. Generally speaking, if your car is ten years old or newer, you should be good to go. If it is ten to fifteen years old, you may be okay depending on what city you are in.

Uber

Uber Service Classes

Driving for Uber can be very lucrative, depending on the car you are driving. Setting itself apart from Lyft and other rideshare competitors, Uber offers several classes of car service. Generally speaking, the more people your car can seat and the more luxurious it is, the higher your pay rate— trust me; you will stand to make quite a bit more money with a large or luxurious car than the average driver will who rolls around in a basic sedan. In the next few sections, I will share Uber's list of service classes and the cars eligible to be in each class. The service classes we'll be discussing in order are: UberX, UberXL, UberSELECT, UberBLACK, UberSUV, UberLUX, and UberPOOL. Please note that not all service classes are available in every city. Generally speaking, though, UberX, UberXL, and UberSELECT are universal across the U.S.

UberX

UberX is the plain Jane, vanilla Uber service most of us recognize. UberX vehicles are four-door sedans that seat five passengers, including the driver. Per the Uber website, recommended UberX vehicles include, but are not limited to:

- Chevrolet: Cruze, Equinox, Impala, Malibu
- Chrysler: 200, 300
- Dodge: Avenger, Dart
- Ford: Focus, Fusion, Edge, Escape
- Honda: Accord, Civic, Element
- Hyundai: Elantra, Sonata, Tucson
- Kia: Optima, Sorento
- Mazda: Mazda3
- Mitsubishi: Lancer
- Nissan: Altima, Sentra

- Toyota: Corolla, Camry, Prius
- Volkswagen: Jetta, Passat
- Volvo: S40, S60

UberXL

UberXL is Uber's deluxe size car service, seating six passengers or more and intended for transporting larger groups. UberXL vehicles are usually larger sedans, trucks, vans, or SUVs. Per Uber's website, recommended UberXL vehicles include, but are not limited to:

- Chevrolet: Traverse
- Chrysler: Town and Country
- Dodge: Durango, Caravan, Journey
- Ford: Explorer, Flex
- GMC: Acadia
- Honda: Odyssey, Pilot
- Hyundai: Santa Fe
- Jeep: Commander
- Kia: Sedona
- Mazda: CX-9

- Mercury: Mountaineer

- Mitsubishi: Outlander

- Nissan: Pathfinder, Quest

- Subaru: Tribeca

- Toyota: Highlander, Sequoia

- Volkswagen: Toureg

UberXL drivers earn higher base, per mile, and per minute rates (on average up to 30 percent more as compared to basic UberX drivers). If you're a soccer family with a mini-van, you are at a distinct advantage!

UberSELECT

UberSELECT is Uber's higher end car service, featuring mid-luxury vehicles such as BMWs, Audis, or Mercedes style cars. SELECT vehicles must have either a leather or vinyl interior and seat five passengers, including the driver. Generally speaking, you can think of it as UberX's upgraded, richer brother. Per the Uber website, SELECT eligible vehicles include:

- Acura: RDX, RLX, TL, TLX, ILX

- Audi: A3, A4, A5, A6, A7, A8, S3, S4, S6, S7, S8,

Q3, Q5, Q7

- BMW: 3-series, 5-series, 7-series, M3, M5, M6, X1, X3, X4, X5, X6
- Cadillac: ATS, CTS, DTS, SRX, XTS
- Hummer: H3
- Infiniti: EX, FX, G, I, M, Q40, Q50, Q60, Q70, QX50, QX56, QX70
- Jaguar: S-Type, X-Type
- Lexus: ES, GS, GX, IS, LS, NX, RX
- Lincoln: MKT, MKS, MKX, MKZ, Town Car
- Mercedes-Benz: C-Class, E-Class, S-Class, GL-Class, G-Class, GLK-Class, M-Class, R-Class
- Porsche: Macan, Cayenne, Panamera
- Tesla: Model S, Model X
- Volvo: S60, S80, XC90

On average, SELECT drivers can make twice as much per ride as their UberX counterparts. If you have a higher class car, rideshare driving can definitely be a lucrative gig for you.

UberBLACK

One step beyond UberSELECT, UberBLACK is Uber's black car service featuring high end, four-door sedans with professional class drivers. UberBLACK drivers must be commercially registered and all cars must have black leather or vinyl interiors and black exteriors. Per the Uber website, UberBLACK eligible vehicles include:

- Audi: A6, Q7
- Cadillac: XTS
- Infiniti: Q70
- Jaguar: XF
- Mercedes-Benz: E-Class

UberBLACK drivers, on average, can make three times as much as their UberX counterparts.

UberSUV

UberSUV is basically UberBLACK except with SUVs. All vehicles must have a black leather or vinyl interior and black exterior. All drivers must be commercially registered. Like UberBLACK, UberSUV is only available in certain markets. Per the Uber website, eligible vehicles include:

- Cadillac: Escalade ESV

- Chevrolet: Suburban

- GMC: Yukon XL

- Infiniti: QX56, QX80

- Lexus: LX

- Lincoln: Navigator L

- Mercedes-Benz: GL-Class

UberSUV drivers stand to make three times the fare of UberX counterparts. Again, if you have an UberSUV eligible vehicle and live in an UberSUV market, definitely check it out!

UberLUX

UberLUX is only offered on a limited basis in certain cities and is Uber's elite car service, offering high-end luxury vehicles. UberLUX's drivers must meet the same requirements as UberBLACK drivers (commercial registration, and all cars must have black leather or vinyl interiors and black exteriors), but they must also drive the most exclusive and premium of vehicles. Per the Uber website, eligible vehicles include:

- Audi: A8

- Bentley: All four-door models

- BMW: 7-series

- Jaguar: XJ

- Land Rover: Range Rover

- Lexus: LS

- Maybach: All four-door models

- Mercedes-Benz: G-Class, S-Class

- Porsche: Panamera

- Rolls Royce: All four-door models

- Tesla: Model S

Going far beyond any service offering in terms of price, UberLUX drivers stand to make a whopping six times the fare of an UberX counterpart. If you have an eligible vehicle and live in a market with UberLUX, you most definitely want to consider looking into becoming an UberLUX driver.

UberACCESS

UberACCESS is available to all drivers who wish to provide service to Americans with disabilities. To become an AC-CESS driver, you simply need to complete a short online training course that provides information on the Americans with Disabilities Act and how to provide service to Americans with disabilities, how to interact with service animals, and how to fold and store a wheelchair properly. UberACCESS is not a car-dependent service but rather driver-based—for all drivers who wish to certify and participate.

UberPOOL

UberPOOL is Uber's passenger matching service that allows passengers heading in the same direction to share a ride at reduced rates. UberPOOL is offered in limited cities. In participating POOL cities, all eligible vehicles are capable of receiving UberPOOL requests. Among the driver community, the POOL service is infamous because drivers do nearly double the work (two pickups and two drop offs) for minimal additional compensation.

Lyft

While not as extensive as Uber's offerings, Lyft does offer three separate classes of service. The basic Lyft service is comparable to UberX service, featuring four-door sedans seating five passengers, including the driver.

Lyft Plus

Lyft Plus is comparable to Uber's XL service, featuring sedans, trucks, SUVs, and vans that seat six or more passengers.

Lyft Line

Lyft Line is comparable to Uber's POOL service, allowing passengers heading in the same direction to share a ride. Like POOL, Lyft Line is available in a limited number of cities. All Lyft vehicles in participating cities are eligible to receive Line requests.

Upgrading Your Car

As noted, drivers who drive cars eligible for UberXL/Lyft Plus or UberSELECT, BLACK, SUV, or LUX (in available markets) stand to make anywhere from three to six times as much as UberX or regular Lyft drivers. The temptation to upgrade or purchase a qualifying car is great, given the potential earnings.

If you are considering purchasing a new car to drive for Uber or Lyft, there are some considerations to weigh before doing so. For many, rideshare driving is a great source of extra income, but like any capital investment or financial decision, you want to gather all the information available before you commit. The last thing you want to do is make a big purchase, take on a lot of debt, and become "stuck" with something that may not work in your situation.

Consider the following before you decide to buy or finance a vehicle that qualifies for XL/Plus, SELECT, BLACK, SUV, or LUX classification:

- **The market for rideshare in your town**. While rideshare driving is a great source of income opportunity in many markets, in smaller markets, opportunities are marginal—user demand may be low, or the market may be saturated with drivers. In these markets, many drivers may struggle to break even. If you're looking at rideshare as your primary, or at least a significant, source of income, be sure you do your research on the demand in your town. You don't want to invest in an expensive, fancy car only to find the demand for that level of service is not there.

- **Prices for rideshare services in your town**. Business is, and always will be, ultimately a numbers game. Find out what the base, mileage, or time rates are for the different classes or rideshare services in your town. For many drivers, the numbers do not work out. In some markets, the base rates and the time and mileage multipliers are minuscule, with short rides paying less than

$5.00 for basic service or $7.00 to $10.00 for XL and up. You need to consider a "worst-case scenario" earning situation to see whether you could still break even on car payments, insurance, and fuel costs. If the numbers don't work, you're in trouble, and you will need to consider other options.

- **Demand for XL/Plus, SELECT, BLACK, SUV, or LUX service**. Yes, you do earn significantly more per ride with the premium platforms, but you need to have a realistic view of the demand for these services. How often will the average person need and be willing to pay for SELECT service when X will get him or her there just fine? You don't necessarily want to invest in a SELECT or better classified vehicle just to find the demand ratio is nine UberX requests to every UberSELECT request.

- **Loan conditions you're able to secure.** What rate are you paying to finance? What is it monthly? At the beginning, Uber partnered with loan companies to offer many subprime loans to drivers with limited or no credit. The deals were horrible, leaving drivers stuck in leases they could barely afford. If you are financing, make sure you get the best deal possible since you don't want to get stuck with a car you can't afford.

- **Stability of Uber, Lyft, and/or rideshare in your town.** How stable is the rideshare industry in your town? Is the cost of meeting strict regulations high? Uber and Lyft have been known to abandon markets where regulations have made the business model unfeasible. Has Uber or Lyft slashed rates in your town recently? Both companies have been known to cut rates to drive up demand (or undercut each other). You don't want to invest heavily in a car only to discover the rideshare company you planned to work for is closing up shop (and leaving you holding the bag); nor do you want to discover the company has cut prices so drastically that you can't earn enough to make your car payments.

Summary

In this chapter, we looked at the various driver programs and car service classes offered by Uber and Lyft. Driving cars that hold more people pays off because UberXL and Lyft Plus earn at least a third more on fares than the standard UberX or Lyft services. Driving a higher end car can pay you anywhere from two to six times more on Uber if you are a SELECT, BLACK, SUV, or LUX driver. Given the potential for higher payout, there is something to be said for considering investing in a higher capacity or higher end vehicle, but any purchase or lease decisions should be weighed against demand and any other market conditions affecting rideshare in your town.

Driving Forward

Let's get you ready for the road by figuring out which services your car is eligible for and whether upgrading your car is a good idea for you.

1. What service classes do Uber and/or Lyft have in your city?

2. What service classes is your car eligible for?

3. Are you considering buying a new car?

4. What rates do Uber or Lyft charge passengers?

5. Has either Uber and/or Lyft adjusted rates in your town recently?

6. Talking with other drivers, what is the demand for premium services

7. If you are considering financing a car, what loan rates are available? What rates do you qualify for?

CHAPTER 5
HOW IT WORKS

"I really enjoy it—it's like a videogame on wheels.
A GPS touch screen is one of the most entertaining
things I've ever seen in a car."

— Mike Shinoda

The Rearview Mirror

In the last chapter, I explained the various driver programs and car service classes offered by Uber and Lyft. Generally speaking, if you can carry more passengers or you drive a high-end vehicle, you stand to make way more money than the average sedan driver. In Chapter 1, I touched briefly on how you get fares. In this chapter, I will walk you through exactly how ridesharing works on a technical level.

DRIVING PROFITS AND MAKING BANK

No Cash

First, let me clarify that one of the beautiful things about the rideshare model is that *no cash* exchanges hands between drivers and riders (unless riders choose to tip you in cash). All rides are billed through the app as riders input their credit card or PayPal information into the system. You as the driver, therefore, don't need to keep cash on hand to make change and you don't need to swipe credit cards at the end of the ride. Taking the cash out of the transaction system makes rideshare driving easy and painless.

Turn on Your App

First and foremost, when you are ready to start driving, you need to turn on the Uber Driver app and/or the Lyft app and go into Driver Mode.

Go "Online"

Once you turn the app on, you will want to Go Online on both apps. When you are Online, all riders see you are available and ready to take ride requests. If you are offline, you are not advertising that you are ready to take requests, and thus, no requests will come your way.

HOW IT WORKS

Get Matched

While Online, you are advertised as being ready to accept rides. You are then matched with the nearest ride requester.

Accept Ride Requests

When a ride request comes in ("pings"), you have the option to accept it (recommended) or to ignore it and let it pass. Typically, the rider's name, pickup location, and passenger rating score will display along with the ride service class (UberX, XL, SELECT, Lyft Plus, etc.). On Uber, it will also display whether Surge pricing (see Chapter 6) is applicable to the fare.

Navigate to Pickup Point

Once you accept a ride request, the app takes over and uses your phone's GPS system to navigate to the pickup point.

Pickup Rider

Upon arrival at the pickup point, the passenger enters your vehicle and you formally swipe or tap "Pickup" passenger—at this point, the ride officially begins.

DRIVING PROFITS AND MAKING BANK

Drop Off Rider

If the passenger has entered a destination into the app (or you have upon his instruction), then once the passenger enters your vehicle and you click "Start Ride," your GPS will take over again, directing you to the drop off point. At the destination, swipe or click "Drop Off" or "End Ride" once the passenger has left your vehicle.

End Ride

Once you have clicked or swiped "Drop Off" or "End Ride," you will be asked to rate the passenger on a scale of one to five. Ratings are mandatory, and you will not be released to the driver pool until you have rated your passenger. Both Uber and Lyft's policies require drivers to rate all passengers as part of the service's internal controls and security system to help ensure only safe and courteous passengers are allowed to remain on the platform. If a passenger's ratings drop below a certain threshhold or there are enough complaints about the person, he or she will be banned from the platform. In addition, you as a driver can also request never to be matched to a particular passenger in the future.

Get Paid

Once you've finished rating your passenger, your earnings receipt for the ride will display.

Summary

In this chapter, we walked through the process of drivers getting matched with passengers, accepting rides, and completing rides. You need to launch the driver apps, "Go Online" to be eligible to receive requests, accept requests as they come in, and navigate to pickup locations. From there, you'll pick up your passengers, use GPS to navigate to their destinations, drop them off, formally end the ride on the app, rate them, and view your pay receipt. It's that simple.

Driving Forward

Let's continue to get you ready to hit the road by looking at the Lyft driver tutorial and configuring your phone's GPS.

1. Play around with the Lyft driver in-app tutorial.

2. Practice using GPS on your phone to navigate.

CHAPTER 6

SURGE AND PRIMETIME PRICING

"The two most important requirements for major success are: first being in the right place at the right time, and second, doing something about it."

— Ray Kroc

The Rearview Mirror

In the last chapter, I walked you through how drivers are matched with riders through the Uber and Lyft apps. In this chapter, I will discuss the much sought-after Surge and Primetime pricings and how they work.

DRIVING PROFITS AND MAKING BANK

Surge and Primetime Areas

In a nutshell, both Uber and Lyft charge premium rates during peak demand to encourage more drivers to get out on the road. Uber calls this "Surge" pricing. Lyft calls it "Primetime" pricing. Consumers probably think of it as price gouging, but a price gouge to them is a big payday for us.

Typically speaking, Surges and Primetimes will always occur at the following times of day: morning rush hour, afternoon rush hour, shift change at retail outlets, hotels, or military installations, flight arrival times at airports, and bar closing times.

In Uber, Surges are displayed in gradients of yellow, orange, and red with multipliers (1.5x, 2.0x, 3.0x, 4.0x, etc.).

In Lyft, Primetimes are displayed in gradients of pink as percentages (100, 150, 200 percent, etc.).

Regular Emails from Uber and Lyft

Because Uber and Lyft stand to make money whenever you make money, they will always contact you either via email or text to coach you on the best times to get on the road. Weekly, you'll receive charts on the best times to drive based on user demand in your area. Often, they'll build in bonus incentives for driving certain hours and pay bonuses for completing a given number of rides during designated times.

Uber staffs a local support office in each market that will also contact and provide information on key times to drive and updates on any upcoming events where driver demand is expected to be high, such as concerts, festivals, or sporting events.

Third Party Apps

Third party apps that collect Surge and Primetime data are available for both the iOS and Android for Uber and Lyft. Using these apps and analyzing the data can help you determine the best places and times to drive. I'll cover this topic in more depth in Chapter 12.

Driving During Surge and Prime Hours

Drivers who drive during major Surge and Primetime periods—and are lucky—can easily earn fares in excess of $100.00, depending on the multiplier applied and the distance of the ride. On weekend evenings, when Surges, Primetimes, and long distance rides are plentiful, it is not uncommon for drivers to earn several hundred dollars over the course of a weekend.

DRIVING PROFITS AND MAKING BANK

Summary

In this chapter, I discussed Surge and Primetime pricing. They are tools used by Uber and Lyft to encourage more drivers to get on the road during peak demand hours. Uber and Lyft will coach you via emails and texts on the best times to drive based on passenger data in your area. Often, they will build incentives into driver rates during certain hours, offering bonuses to complete a certain number of rides during peak hours. Third party apps are available for iOS and Android to help you capture and analyze data on the best times and locations to drive. If you are lucky, it is not uncommon to catch fares in excess of $100.00 due to Surge or Primetime pricing for longer distance rides.

Driving Forward

Let's continue to get you ready for the road by helping you find and analyze Surge and Primetime data.

1. Check the iOS or Google Play Stores for Surge or Primetime tracking apps and download them.
2. Play with the apps and note peaks hours and locations in your area.
3. Study any email you get from Uber or Lyft detailing Surge and Primetime hours.

4. Note what the prime hours and locations are and how they fit into your schedule.

CHAPTER 7
HOW YOU MAKE MONEY

"Show me the money!"

— Jerry Maguire

The Rearview Mirror

In the last chapter, I talked about Surge and Primetime pricing, which can help you boost your earnings significantly and is probably the most popular way drivers make money. In this chapter, I will discuss additional items built into the system to help you earn money.

Ride Fares

The most basic way you'll earn money as a driver, as you would expect, is to give rides. Much like a taxi cab ride, fares are determined by a basic formula:

$$Base\ Rate + Distance(x) + Time(x)$$

This can be boosted if you are fortunate and catch a Surge or Primetime fare. At the time of publication, Uber was taking 25 percent of all fares and Lyft took 20 percent. Base rates vary by city and by service class (XL/Plus, SELECT, etc.). Some cities offer drivers a minimum guarantee, due to low base rates.

Driver Referrals

Probably the next most popular method of earning money off the platform is referring new drivers (i.e., your friends and family) to sign up as fellow drivers. Both Uber and Lyft provide you with a referral code visible in your app and on a driver dashboard on the web that you can share via email, text, or social media to encourage new drivers to sign up. In many cities, Uber and Lyft offer generous and extended promotions to get new drivers onboard via current driver referral. Normal referral rates average about $100–$200 once a referral completes a minimum required number of rides (usually between thirty to fifty rides in a month). In many cities, Uber and Lyft also offer deluxe editions of these promotions, paying several hundred dollars for multiple referrals.

Passenger Referrals

The final method for making cash from the ridesharing platform is new passenger referrals. Not everyone wants to be a driver, but *everyone* can use a good, affordable, and safe ride, whether it's for a night out on the town, because the car is in the shop, or while traveling. You can earn cash or ride credits (even as a passenger, you don't need to drive!) by sharing your passenger sign-up referral link via text, email, or social media. The average referral bonus is $10–$20 in cash or ride credits. At the time of this writing, Lyft pays cash bonuses, while Uber gives ride credits. Referral rates vary from city to city.

Rates Vary by City

Again, to reiterate, driving rates and referral rates for new drivers and new passengers vary by city. Check your city page on the Uber or Lyft website for alerts on current rates and referral promotions in your town.

DRIVING PROFITS AND MAKING BANK

Share Your Referral Codes

Get your bonus promotions! Share your referral codes like a fiend! Post them to all your social media. Text or email your invitation codes to family and friends looking for additional income who enjoy driving! Text or email your codes to all your friends leaving for a trip or who have a car in the shop. The more you share and refer, the more you earn.

Summary

In this chapter, I discussed the three ways Uber and Lyft pay you: your ride fares, driver referral fees, and passenger referral fees. Rates and promotions vary by city, so you should check your city pages to find current rates and promotions. You should regularly share your referral codes on social media and with family and friends whom you think may need them.

Driving Forward

Let's get you earning some referral money!

1. Think of ten friends you can refer as new drivers.

2. Think of ten friends you can refer as new passengers.

CHAPTER 8
GETTING PAID

"I'll be truthful. The weekly paycheck is the
most important thing to me."

— Bela Lugosi

The Rearview Mirror

In the last chapter, I talked about the three ways you can make
money as an Uber or Lyft driver: ride fares, driver referrals, and
passenger referrals. In this chapter, I will discuss exactly when
and how you get paid.

Standard Weekly Deposit

When you signed up as a driver, you were required to enter

your bank information into the app or website. This is because Uber and Lyft will deposit your earnings each and every week into your bank account via direct deposit. Yes! This is a weekly paycheck—at minimum!

With weekly earnings you can rest assured, knowing you have continuous cash flow to help meet your financial obligations. No more waiting two weeks and praying your money does not run out!

Daily Pay Options

If weekly payouts are too infrequent for you, you can take advantage of daily pay options and services!

Lyft innovated this service with its "Quick Pay" option, which allows you to cash out your earnings, provided you've earned and have at least $50 in unpaid earnings! For this convenience, you do pay a convenience fee. The earnings will be deposited to your debit card, which you must input to enable Quick Pay.

Uber followed suit with a similar service in mid-2016, allowing direct cash out to your bank card for a nominal fee. In early 2016, Uber partnered with GoBank to allow daily cash out to a GoBank account. Prior to this, a third party also facilitated daily cash outs from Uber.

No matter what service you use, daily cash outs provide major convenience in terms of helping with cash flow.

Summary

In this chapter, I discussed how and where you get paid your driver earnings. As a standard, Uber and Lyft both pay on a weekly basis. For a nominal fee, you can withdraw earnings on a daily basis from Uber. You can withdraw from Lyft daily as well, provided you have at least $50 of undrawn earnings and pay the convenience fee. With its quick pay options, rideshare driving provides strong cash flow opportunities for drivers beyond the standard two-week pay cycle common in America.

Driving Forward

Let's get your cash flow running to the positive by examining your bills, obligations, and the daily pay options available at Uber and Lyft.

1. Look into the daily pay options for both Lyft and Uber. Examine any associated fees or costs of these pay options.

2. Examine your own schedule of bills and analyze your

cash flow to see on which days certain bills need to be paid.

3. Do you plan to cash out daily, use the daily pay as needed, or stick to the standard, weekly paycheck?

CHAPTER 9
INSURANCE COVERAGE

"I am prepared for the worst but hope for the best."

— Benjamin Disraeli

The Rearview Mirror

In the last chapter, I talked about Uber and Lyft's pay schedule and payout options. In this chapter, I will talk about driver insurance requirements.

Coverages and Periods

Uber and Lyft both cover all rides taken and performed while on their clock. Semantics wise, you'll hear things such as Period 1, Period 2, and Period 3 coverage. Period 1 refers to the time the app is on but you have not accepted a rider. Period 2 refers to the period during which you've accepted a rider and you are en route to a pickup. Period 3 refers to the time when you are actively driving a passenger to his or her destination.

Fancy semantics aside, basically, what you need to know is that Uber and Lyft fully insure you from the time you accept a ride request until the time you drop a passenger off (Period 2 and Period 3. During Period 1, when the app is on but you've not accepted a rider, you are on your own, under your own personal coverage.

Uber's Coverage

Uber's coverage is offered through the James River Insurance Company. A copy of the certificate is available both in the driver Uber app and on the Uber website. Note that the insured party on the certificate is Rasier, LLC, which is the Uber subsidiary that all independent contracts are with. You'll notice all of your driver agreements are with Rasier, LLC. It's recommended that you print a copy of this certificate and keep it in your car with your personal insurance policy.

Lyft's Coverage

Lyft's policy is available in the app under Settings—Vehicles—Lyft Insurance. It is also available for download from the Lyft website. Lyft's insurer is the Steadfast Insurance Company. It's recommended that you print out and keep a copy of this policy alongside your personal insurance policy.

Personal Insurance Coverage

Under company policy, you must maintain personal coverage on your vehicle to be eligible to be a driver. Personal coverage is also the law in most states and jurisdictions.

Local Law Requirements

As the rideshare industry becomes more regulated, many jurisdictions will require rideshare drivers to keep additional insurance beyond personal policies, be it commercial driver insurance or additional rideshare riders to your personal policy. Insurance companies are responding to the change in regulations, and many are starting to offer rideshare policies. Check your city page on the Uber or Lyft websites for current laws and requirements.

DRIVING PROFITS AND MAKING BANK

Caution on Personal Insurance

A brief word of caution on personal insurance. Not all states offer rideshare-friendly policies, and for many insurance companies, rideshare driving is frowned upon due to the liability involved. Many insurance companies in states without rideshare insurance requirements have canceled policies upon learning clients are rideshare drivers. It is recommended you check with your insurance company about its rideshare driving policies if you're interested in becoming a driver. The Rideshare Guy blog (www.therideshareguy.com) offers a great list of insurance companies and states with rideshare-friendly insurance policies.

Summary

In this chapter, I discussed the issue of insurance coverage. Both Uber and Lyft will insure you from the time you accept a ride request until you drop off your passenger. Insurance certificates for both Uber and Lyft are available on the app and their websites. You should print copies and keep them with your personal insurance card. Local laws may dictate additional insurance requirements beyond your personal policy. Check your city's pages at Uber or Lyft or check with your local government for any insurance requirements you must adhere to as a rideshare driver.

Driving Forward

Let's get you ready for the road by getting you insured so you can drive with piece of mind and be covered in the event of an accident.

1. Download and print copies of the Uber and Lyft insurance certificates for your state and put these copies in your vehicle.

2. Research the insurance requirements for rideshare drivers in your city—Uber and Lyft websites are a good starting point.

PART II
LIFE AS A DRIVER

CHAPTER 10
STAYING DRIVER ELIGIBLE

"Another way to lose control is to ignore something when you should address it."

— Jim Evans

The Rearview Mirror

In previous chapters, I talked about the basics of being a rideshare driver, including the sign-up process, eligibility requirements for drivers and vehicles, and how the service works. In this part of the book, I will discuss life as a rideshare driver. In this particular chapter, I will explain how to maintain driver eligibility, including what can cause drivers to be deactivated, and how to remain a top-notch driver.

DRIVING PROFITS AND MAKING BANK

Maintaining Your Driver Ratings

Aside from illegal activities, the main cause of drivers losing their eligibility is having their ratings drop below acceptable levels. For both Uber and Lyft, you must maintain at least a 4.70 rating. If your rating falls below 4.70, your account is flagged for scrutiny, and if your ratings don't improve, you risk being deactivated. You may then be asked to complete a driver training program to help learn ways to improve your ratings, to avoid deactivation, or to earn reinstatement.

In the next few sections, I will go over some of the things you are evaluated on by passengers whether you drive for Uber or Lyft.

Safety

By and large, safety is the most important standard to which all drivers are held. You should always practice safe driving habits, including:

- adhering to the speed limit and traffic laws

- not weaving in and out of traffic

- not driving under the influence of drugs or alcohol

- not being distracted by texting while driving

- not talking on your phone without a hands-free set

Always practice safe driving for your safety, your passengers' safety, and the safety of others on the road.

If you are an unsafe driver, passengers will most definitely notice, and it will be reflected in your ratings.

Professionalism

You are also rated on professionalism. You should always treat passengers with courtesy, respect, and friendliness.

Drivers who make polite conversation are usually rated higher because they provide a pleasant experience. Use caution and avoid conversation that is invasive or personal. You'll need to maintain a friendly, personable demeanor, and avoid being creepy, probing, or inappropriate.

Finally, avoid turning your car into a driving infomercial. Many drivers may use the opportunity to promote other services they offer (real estate, insurance, multi-level marketing). This practice is discouraged. There are opportunities to promote other services you offer, but there's a right way and a wrong way of doing it. Turning your ride into a driving infomercial, where you come straight out and ask passengers whether they'd be interested in your other services or opportunities, and having that dominate the entire conversation, is most definitely the wrong, unprofessional way. If you would like to use your rideshare platform to promote your services, I will offer you some tips for doing so in Chapter 26.

Cleanliness

Another standard that drivers are held to and rated on is the cleanliness of their vehicles. I'm sure we've all been in dirty cars or cabs. It's not a pleasant experience.

Work to keep your car as clean as possible inside and out. Here are some tips:

- Vacuum, sweep, and dust the seats and floors daily. Invest in a good car vacuum if you don't have one already.

- Wipe down the interior with surface wipes.

- Keep stuff off the seats and floors. If you've used your car as storage or a filing cabinet, you'll need to find other places to keep or store your stuff.

- Keep your trunk as clear and clean as possible. Many passengers, including tourists and business travelers, are heading to the airport. You don't want to lose out on a good fare because you did not have enough room for luggage.

- Use a car scent/air freshener. It'll make the riding experience much more pleasant for you and your riders.

- Don't smoke or allow others to smoke in your car. The smoke smell lingers and can upset passengers.

Simply put, clean cars equal happy riders, positive reviews, and better earnings.

Navigation

Navigation is the final criteria you are evaluated on. We've all been on cab rides where the driver either takes the scenic route or simply gets lost. If you're a tourist or a newcomer in town, you may not know whether or not the driver is going the long way. With ridesharing, taking the most direct and efficient route possible is what is most valued. The Uber and Lyft apps are built to work with your phone's GPS app (Waze, Google Maps, etc.), so navigation should be a fairly easy criteria to nail. Always use the GPS to navigate.

Occasionally, though, some passengers may have their preferred routes and will let you know. Customers are always right, so if they have routes they wish to take, oblige them.

In a nutshell, always use the GPS to navigate to pickups and during rides unless the passenger asks you to take an alternate route.

Acceptance and Cancellation Rates

Two other things are taken into consideration when Uber and Lyft evaluate driver partners: acceptance rates and cancellation rates.

Acceptance rates refer to the number of ride requests you accept. Low acceptance rates are frowned upon and used to contribute to drivers being deactivated. Because the app matches riders with the closest driver, if drivers do not accept requests, riders have to wait longer. In the past, many drivers wouldn't accept requests for various reasons. The most common reasons for not accepting a ride are being sent non-surge ride requests (drivers holding out for surge requests), the pickup point is too far away (distance or drive time), or your car is eligible for higher end services (XL, SELECT or Plus) so you are holding out for a higher level request.

Due to recent court cases and rulings, acceptance rates will no longer factor in decisions to deactivate you as a partner, but low rates are still frowned upon and can cause you to be logged off and locked out of the Uber Partner app for a certain number of minutes. If your rate is low, both Uber and Lyft will start to send you e-mails or text messages encouraging you to accept more incoming rides.

"Cancellation rate" refers to the number of rides you, as the driver, cancel once you've accepted a ride request. Canceled requests do and will count against you, and an excessive number of cancelled requests can lead to deactivation. The rationale is, once again, based on passenger service and convenience. When drivers cancel accepted rides and leave passengers waiting, it extends wait time. Things do come up that necessitate cancelling a pickup, but cancellations should be kept to a minimum and always have good cause, not be arbitrary. Note that when you do cancel a ride, the app will give you a list of reasons why you canceled the trip. Some reasons are necessary and won't be held against you (i.e., passenger no show, too many passengers at the pickup, luggage did not fit, passenger asked you to cancel the ride, etc.).

As a driver, I typically do not accept ride requests if the rider is more than thirty minutes from my location (as determined by GPS estimate). This is more common on Lyft than on Uber. Requests that far away may be of lower margin, especially if the rider only plans to go a short distance. And the rider may be better served repeating the request and catching a closer driver. If I do accept an incoming long distance request, I will call the rider to see where he or she is heading. (Neither Uber or Lyft's platforms will tell you where the rider wants to go; consequently, that means you may drive thirty minutes to pick up someone, who only wants a five-minute ride, but that is a chance you take; I get around this situation by calling the rider to make sure it's worth my while.) If the distance is long enough and I think it's worth my time and expense, I'll fulfill the request. If the ride sounds too short and not worth my time or expense, I'll ask the rider to cancel and re-request in hopes of getting a closer driver.

With regards to holding out for Surge requests, you can try to time the Surges and Primetimes with the use of third-party apps or toggling back and forth between the driver and rider apps. In these instances, you may choose to go offline to avoid adversely affecting your acceptance rates if you plan to pass on non-surge or lower level rides. When I get a non-Surge request around what should normally be a Surge time in my area, depending on how the night is going, I may let it pass, knowing I'll get a Surge soon. For example, if I get a request at 1:50 a.m. that isn't a surge, and I know the Surge period starts at 2:00 a.m. when the bars close, I may let it pass. On slow nights, however, I may accept the non-Surge request because something is better than nothing.

By and large, though, do your best to accept the majority of ride requests and only cancel rides if necessary.

Don't Commit Crimes

A final consideration and evaluation criteria Uber and Lyft use to determine whether a driver should be deactivated is whether or not you commit a crime against a passenger. It should go without saying, but do not be a criminal!

Over the years, there have been high profile news stories about rideshare drivers who have assaulted, robbed, kidnapped, or raped passengers. There have also been stories about drivers who, after picking up passengers from their homes and dropping them off at the airport, later returned to the now empty home to burglarize it. Needless to say, all of these drivers were deactivated as partners and all went to jail/prison.

Don't be a criminal and victimize your riders. That's totally not cool.

Summary

In this chapter, I talked about the criteria used to rate drivers. Drivers are rated by their passengers on safety while driving, professionalism, cleanliness of the vehicle, and navigation abilities. Uber and Lyft also take into consideration acceptance and cancellation rates. Driver partners should accept and complete the majority of ride requests.

Driving Forward

Complete the following tasks to help you get on the road and set yourself up for success as a driver—and to keep yourself activated through exceptional service.

1. Get a phone mount if you don't have one already. Safety first.

2. Set up a car cleaning schedule. How often and when will you wipe down or vacuum your car's interior? Daily? Three times a week? How often will you wash your car? Once a week? Every two weeks?

3. Purchase any equipment and supplies necessary to keep your car clean (vacuum, service wipes, soap, etc.).

4. Choose and install a GPS system on your phone if you don't already have or use one.

CHAPTER 11

RIDESHARE PEOPLE

"The first step in exceeding your customer's expectations is to know those expectations."

— Roy H. Williams

The Rearview Mirror

In the last chapter, I talked about driver ratings, the criteria on which drivers are evaluated, and how you can maintain strong ratings. In this chapter, I will shift our focus to the common passenger types you'll encounter as a driver. Knowing the types of passengers you'll be serving can help you to customize and maximize a great rider experience, helping you keep your ratings up and earn return business.

DRIVING PROFITS AND MAKING BANK

Tourists

Predictably, you will be driving a lot of tourists around. As a driver, you'll typically get requests from them from airports, hotel districts, and other tourist attractions and hot spots.

Tourists appreciate recommendations on places to visit or dine. Do your best to know the following:

- great restaurants for particular cuisine styles
- great hole in the wall restaurants
- family attractions
- scenic attractions
- cultural or historical attractions
- nightlife hotspots

Great suggestions for visitors will equal great reviews on the app, tip money, and potential return business.

Business Travelers

You will encounter many business travelers. This category of rider is typically in town to work with clients or for conferences. You will typically encounter them at airports, convention centers, hotel districts, or university areas. Much like tourists, they too will appreciate tips on places to eat or visit during their downtime from work. As with tourists, great information will lead to great reviews, tip potential, and potential repeat business.

Daily Commuters

One of the surprising things I found when I first started driving was the high number of people who commute to their jobs daily via Uber or Lyft. For many commuters, rideshare commuting makes more financial sense than owning and operating a vehicle, and it is infinitely more convenient than public transportation.

Throughout my time as a rideshare driver, I've picked up and dropped off riders in all industries at all shift times during the day: business people, retail workers, food service workers, hotel workers, healthcare workers, security workers, military personnel, etc. I've picked up folks working all shifts—day, swing, or graveyard. If you drive the same times each day in the same areas, there's a good chance you'll develop regulars.

By driving in a major metropolitan area, I've been fortunate to drive all hours of the day and see consistent demand from commuters at all hours. I've driven during morning rush hour, taking commuters to work. I've driven during evening rush hour, taking commuters home. In the afternoons, I've taken swing shift workers to work, and late at night, I've taken swing shift workers home while dropping graveyard shift workers off at work.

DRIVING PROFITS AND MAKING BANK

If targeting shift workers, you'll want to get a good feel for business or retail districts that have long hours and be aware of when shift changes happen so you can capitalize on taking workers home.

In particular, swing shift workers getting off and graveyard shift workers going to work will almost always request rides because public transportation is not as reliable or does not run as often during those hours. You'll always find workers between the hours of 10 p.m. and 2 a.m. needing rides to and from work in retail districts (sales staff), hotel districts (desk, housekeeping, valet, retail), restaurant/bar districts (kitchen and wait staff), hospitals (nurses and technicians), and condominium, housing, business, and industrial complexes (security guards).

College Students

College students represent a good percentage of regular ride requesters. We've all been there ourselves at some point in our lives: poor and carless.

You'll regularly get ride requests from college residence halls, campuses, or communities surrounding college campuses.

Typically, college kids will need rides to or from classes, to home or jobs, or to do grocery runs or other errands. On the weekends, college residence halls come alive with requests to go to nightclubs or bars in the community.

Military Members and Dependents

Similar to college students who are often carless and need to get to and from campus, military bases and housing areas are also full of service members and their dependents, many of whom are also carless and need to get to and from work and around the community. During my time as a rideshare driver, I've driven hundreds of service members to and from base, to bars and nightclubs, and simply to and from work. The same is true with their family members who also need rides to and from home, work, school, and the base exchange or commissary.

One thing to note about military bases is that they are secured areas, and depending on the base command, you may need credentials to enter them. If the base you are serving is particularly strict, you may need to ask riders to meet you at the gate or let your passengers going to base know that they may need to walk from the base gate to their deslination. In my area, we have three bases. Two will allow drivers on for drop offs and (with a guest pass) pickups. The other base will not grant us access without proper military or government ID.

DRIVING PROFITS AND MAKING BANK

Older Residents

Another common category of riders you will encounter are the elderly—usually single and living alone, they are carless and need rides to run errands or see the doctor.

Some of these riders are not technologically savvy, so the ride request itself may come from a younger family member (child or grandchild) requesting you to take a parent or grandparent to the grocery store or an appointment.

In my experience, these passengers will typically tip you very well for your help, and you may be able to develop a good relationship with them if they become recurring riders.

Weekend Partiers

By and large, the most lucrative passengers you will come across are the weekend and nighttime party crowd. Weekend evenings are typically the busiest nights of the week, and they rack up the highest Surge and Primetime prices.

On nights like these, you will be running continuous loops between the same bars and nightclubs and the surrounding residential areas, college residence halls, and military bases or housing units. It's been a long work and school week for these people, so they are ready to blow off some steam and have some fun.

On nights like this, be prepared for some lucrative rides throughout the night, with the highest Surges and Primetimes occurring near bar closing time.

This pattern repeats to a lesser extent during the work week for those who are off on week nights and choose to go to bars or nightclubs. For these riders, be prepared for fun high energy conversations. On the downside, keep barf bags handy.

Drunks

Aside from tourists and commuters, much of your ridership will be drunks needing a ride home at the end of the night (or the wee hours of the morning).

This is good and bad. We all know drunk people. Some people handle their alcohol very well and are very fun to be around. Some people don't handle their alcohol well at all and can be very obnoxious.

On the good side, drunk people need to get home, so many will be willing to pay the high Surge and Primetime fees to get there in one piece. If they live far from the bar or nightclub, these rides will be incredibly lucrative—you'll be making very good pay for providing the very valuable service of keeping drunks off the road and getting them home safely.

On the bad side, if your drunk passenger can't handle alcohol well, you may be spending a very long ten minutes, half hour, or more getting them home. In really bad cases, you may be cleaning up a nasty mess in your backseat. And in very, very bad cases, you may need to call a cop for assistance.

During my time as a driver, I've been very lucky. Out of hundreds of drunks, I've typically had a blast laughing along with them (or at them) as we made our merry way down the highway, and I've only had a few instances where they were so obnoxious I couldn't wait to get them out of my car. I've been very fortunate never to need to clean up vomit yet (I keep barf bags handy for them), and I've never needed to deal with a violent drunk.

Summary

In this chapter, I discussed the main categories of riders you'll be dealing with, from vacationing tourists to business travelers, commuters, college students, military service members and their dependents, older residents, and weekend or evening partiers. Knowing the types of riders you're dealing with and the unique needs they each have can help you to interact with and meet their needs better, earning you strong ratings, good tips, and potential return business.

Driving Forward

Grow your earnings and business by thinking about the various categories of passengers you'll be interacting with and how you can provide a positive experience and true value to them.

1. How can you interact with tourists to make a ride more valuable to them?

2. How can you interact with military service members and their dependents to make a ride more valuable to them?

3. How can you interact with college students to make a ride more valuable to them?

4. How can you interact with older residents to make a ride more valuable to them?

5. How can you interact with commuters to make a ride more valuable to them?

CHAPTER 12

KNOWING THE PULSE OF THE TOWN

"You must know the battleground. You must know the time of battle. You can travel a thousand miles and still win the battle."

— Sun Tzu

The Rearview Mirror

In the last chapter, I shared profiles of the most common types of riders you'll be dealing with. In this chapter, I will build on this important concept by helping you understand the need to get a feel for the pulse of your city. Where are things happening? When are things happening? If you can get a feel for where to be and when to be there, you'll be able to get the most lucrative riders at the most lucrative times.

Know the Hot Places

As I alluded to in the last chapter with the rider profiles, you need to know where the hot spots are for rides.

Tourists

Tourists will be one of your most consistent income sources, especially if you're driving during the daytime. You'll find tourists at the following places: airports, hotel and tourist districts, major tourist attractions, and tourist shopping districts. If you don't know them all already, get to know all of the following major tourist attractions or areas in your city:

- theme parks
- adventure parks
- museums
- family attractions and entertainment centers
- hiking trails

- major beaches
- high-end retail areas and tourist shopping districts

Become familiar with the hotel and tourist districts, the major roads there, and the locations of the major hotels. With the growth of the sharing economy, you will also notice many travelers using Airbnb, which will take you to various homes, apartments, and condominium complexes in your community. By and large, though, most tourists still opt for traditional accommodations in the various hotels and hostels in your tourist district. Finally, become familiar with the airport area and the locations of the major car rental centers.

Business Travelers

Business travelers will have similar needs to tourists. Know the area around the airport and the major hotel districts. Coupled with these, know the various convention centers in your town and the surrounding area. Many business travelers are in town for conventions. Also know the business districts, hospitals, and industrial or manufacturing areas. These travelers will always need rides to and between their business appointments, meals, and hotels or other housing accommodations (many use Airbnb).

DRIVING PROFITS AND MAKING BANK

University and Colleges

Carless college students need rides from home to campus, or if living on campus, to off-campus entertainment venues. Throughout the week, you'll be shuttling students from classes to home or to their part-time jobs. On the weekends, residence halls become popular request spots as students look to get off campus to enjoy the nightlife. Holidays and the end-of-term sees thousands of students on residential campuses in need of rides from campus to the airport. Get to know the following in your city:

- the locations of all colleges and universities
- the locations of campus residence halls
- campus sports venues
- communities surrounding college campuses where students tend to live

Military

The United States military employs thousands of service members and civilian employees who all need to commute to work each day. Service members with families live on base, in off-base military housing, or within your community, and like everyone else, all need to get to work, to school, to doctors' appointments, or to run daily errands and to enjoy leisure activities. The military market is always a lucrative market.

Get to know all of the following in your city:

- the locations of all the military bases and their policies on base access for rideshare drivers
- all military housing communities
- the locations of the exchanges (PX/BX/NEX/MCX/CGX) and commissaries

Daily Commuters

Everybody has a job. Everybody needs to get to his or her workplace. As mentioned earlier, thousands of commuters in your town may live close enough to work to choose to commute via rideshare in lieu of owning and operating a vehicle or taking less convenient public transportation. You'll be taking residents from their homes to their places of work in business districts, tourist districts, retail centers, industrial areas, and hospitals and at the end of their shifts back to their homes. Get to know the locations of the following in your city:

- major business centers and districts

- hotel and tourist districts

- major shopping malls, retail centers, and retail districts

- industrial areas

- major hospitals

You can just about always count on a ride request from one of these spots. During lulls in ride requests, head toward one of these areas to wait for a new request to come in.

Weekend and Night Partiers

One of your most lucrative markets as a driver will be "the drunks" and partiers going out on weekends and in the evening. Everyone needs a safe ride home after a night of partying, and these folks pay a premium for that. Get to know the following in your city:

- the locations of all major nightclubs

- the bar districts and the bars within them

- major concert venues

- major sports venues

KNOWING THE PULSE OF THE TOWN

Know the Hot Times

Knowing the right places to be is half the equation. Knowing the right times is equally important in helping you catch the demand and the respective Surges and Primetimes. In this section, I will share my tips for being in the right place at the right time.

Tourists

As mentioned earlier, tourists need rides to and from airports, to and from their accommodations, and to and from various attractions. To help yourself be in the right places at the right times, know the following:

- Flight arrivals and departure times for major airlines. Arrival and departure times are fairly regular each day, so get a feel for daily arrivals of certain airlines.

- Ship arrivals and departures if you live in a cruise ship port city.

- Opening and closing times for major tourist attractions.

Knowing these times can put you in the right place at the right time. Being at popular attractions at closing time will definitely net you tourists needing rides back to their hotels. The farther the attraction is from the hotel areas, the better the fare. Being in the hotel districts two to three hours before scheduled flight departures can put you in the right place at the right time to take travelers from their hotels to the airport. Being near the hotels at the start of the day will put you in the right place to take tourists to attractions for opening times. Being at the airport or port within a few minutes of scheduled arrivals will put you in the right place to take travelers to their hotels.

Universities and Colleges

For college students, get to know when classes start and end. Students will need rides to campus the hour before classes start and rides immediately after classes end if they need to get to jobs or head home.

Major universities also host various sporting events and other entertainment, such as concerts. These events attract large numbers of event goers from the community who flock to campus for games and shows.

Get to know the following:

- class start and end times on the various campuses

- sports venues on campus and game schedules
- entertainment venues on campus and show schedules

Military

Like the rest of us, military members and their families need to get to work, to school, and to various destinations within the community.

Get to know all of the following in your city to best work with our military families:

- the locations of all the military bases and shift change times
- the operating hours of the exchanges (PX/BX/NEX/MCX/CGX) and commissaries

Daily Commuters

We all need to get to work on a daily basis. Knowing when shift changes occur in the various industries in your community will help put you in the right place at the right time. Most people work the typical nine-to-five job, which puts us all on the road during typical morning and afternoon rush hours.

DRIVING PROFITS AND MAKING BANK

You can pick up some lucrative fares being in the right place at the right time for those who work swing and graveyard shifts. This is particularly true for hotel and hospital workers who work day, swing, and graveyard shifts—and retail and restaurant workers who work day and swing shifts. To take advantage of this opportunity, you should know:

- hotel and tourist districts and associated shift change times
- major shopping malls, retail centers, and retail districts and the usual opening times, shift change times, and closing times
- major hospitals and their shift change times

Aside from morning and afternoon rush hours, you will typically catch workers going to and from home for swing and graveyard shifts between the hours of 10 p.m. and 2 a.m. If driving during the day, you'll catch retail and restaurant workers commuting to mid-shift jobs between the hours of 10 a.m. and 1 p.m., and to evening shift jobs during peak traffic starting around 2 p.m. until 4 p.m.

Weekend and Night Partiers

Every weekend evening, scores of people flock to the bars

and nightclubs in your town. Folks who need to decompress will flock to the bars more frequently. Vacationers will hit up the hottest clubs and bars in town.

On weekends and, occasionally, weekday evenings, the various sports venues in your town will host the biggest high school, college, or professional sporting events, and concert venues will host the hottest local, regional, national, or international music or comedy acts.

Get to know the following to get revelers to and from home safely:

- opening and closing times for all major bars and nightclubs
- all bar and nightclub districts
- all sports venues and their schedule of events
- all concert venues and their schedule of events

Bad Weather

Bad weather will also increase rider demand. No one enjoys being stuck on a sidewalk in the rain or during a snowstorm. People who normally catch public transportation are more likely to request a ride if the weather is bad. Pay attention to weather forecasts. If the forecast calls for storms or other bad weather, be prepared for high Surge and Primetime rates and more rides.

Area Saturation

One of the quirks of rideshare driving is the cyclical saturation of the driver market. Both Uber and Lyft continually recruit new drivers with bonus promotions. One side effect is occasionally you will see a downturn in business—the occasional slow days or slow nights. Slow days or nights can usually be attributed to high driver saturation (lots of new drivers have been recruited and have started recently) or other causes such as a tourist off season.

Checking the rider app regularly during downtimes can help you identify whether or not the area you are driving in is saturated with too many drivers.

If you check the rider app and notice lots of other drivers on the road, you'll know you're in a saturated area. If this is the case, one strategy could be to move on to another part of town in a hot area. If the rider app doesn't show a lot of drivers, you can take it as an indication that it is indeed a low demand day (for whatever reason) and move on to another hot area for potential rides. If business is slow, you can always opt to take an extended break and go do something else like hit the gym, the mall, the beach, the movies, or take a meal break and try again later. (Ahh, the joys of being your own boss!)

Checking the Rider App

Uber maintains separate apps for Driver Partners (Uber Partner app) and riders (Uber app). If you're a veteran Uber rider, you'll know how it works. Use the rider app to see how many cars are in your current area and in other areas in which you could potentially wait for riders. If your current area is oversaturated (and thus business is slow), use the app to check other potential hot areas and adjust your location accordingly.

Lyft has one app in which you can toggle between *driver* and *rider* modes. As with the Uber app, Lyft rider mode allows you to see where all drivers are in your area. Moving the pin around will allow you to see driver saturation in given areas. If you're in an oversaturated area, check other areas and make adjustments accordingly.

Short Rides vs. Long Rides

One quirk of the job you will quickly become familiar with as you start to feel the pulse of the town is the phenomenon of "continuous quick, short rides" vs. "occasional long rides."

In my experience, the vast majority of rides are between five and ten minutes and within a certain high concentration area. Typically, in a good hour you will constantly catch these five to ten minute rides (with five to ten minute en route windows to pick up the passenger) for an overall trip that takes between ten to twenty minutes. In a given hour, if you can get back to back trips, you can average three trips.

Occasionally, you will score a "long trip" that will take you anywhere from thirty minutes to an hour of actual "on trip" time. This trip, however, may take you away from high demand areas.

Typically speaking, these longer trips can pay as much in one trip as you would typically make in an hour (or more), but if you get stuck in a low demand area after the drop off, you may wind up waiting a whole hour for a rider or spending that hour driving back to a higher demand area. Knowing your town helps—if you do get stuck in a more rural area, you can make your way to a nearby retail area, college campus, military base, or tourist attraction in hopes of getting a request.

A case in point from my own experience…. I was lucky enough to get a ride request from a tourist going back to his hotel, which was an hour away from the attraction he was visiting. This one-hour trip earned me as much as I would normally make in two hours of regular trips. I was elated! Once that trip ended, though, I was stuck at a rural resort waiting for a return request. A whole forty-five minutes went by with no request. Knowing the area well enough, I started to make my way back to civilization, heading toward one of the military bases. Sure enough, a request came in that took me back even closer to a high demand area. In that second hour, though, I only had that one request, earning me a fraction of what I normally earn in a typical hour. After dropping off the military member, I headed to a popular retail center in one of the suburbs and got a request that took me back to the main part of town. Over the course of a four-hour period, I earned the following:

Hour 1: Double my usual hourly take (long trip from town to rural resort)

Hour 2: A quarter of my usual hourly take (one trip from a military base to a suburb)

Hour 3: My usual hourly take (one medium trip from a suburban retail center to an urban core)

At the end, everything balanced out, but it goes to show you the decisions you will need to make, occasionally, between *waiting things out* or *moving on to better fishing*.

DRIVING PROFITS AND MAKING BANK

Summary

In this chapter, I discussed getting to know the pulse of your town to put yourself in the right places at the right times. I discussed the most common ride request areas per passenger profile. I also discussed peak request times and the need to know things such as job shift change times, opening and closing times for businesses (retail stores, restaurants, bars, and nightclubs), and flight and ship arrival and departure times. I also discussed driver saturation, how you can use the rider app to get a feel for driver saturation, and how knowing your town can help you find riders should you find yourself stuck in a rural area after a long trip.

Driving Forward

Take some time to map out and get to know the pulse of your town! Research the following information to help you get to know all the right places to be in your town and the right times to be there.

1. Note where the airport is and the typical pattern of flight schedules.

2. Note where the hotel districts are and when shift changes occur.

3. Note where all the major tourist attractions are and their hours.

4. Note where all the college campuses in your town are and typical class times.

5. Note where the major shopping centers, malls, and retail districts are and their operating hours.

6. Note where all the military bases are and when shift changes occur.

7. Check the Uber and Lyft rider apps and scroll the pin around town each hour for a week. Note the locations and times when there is driver saturation. Note where and when the Surges and Primetimes occur.

8. Track the Surges and Primetimes each hour near the following places: the airport, tourist attractions, hotel districts, military bases, college campuses, and major retail centers.

CHAPTER 13

HICCUPS OF THE SYSTEM

"An effective way to test code is to exercise it at its natural boundaries."

— Brian Kernighan

The Rearview Mirror

In the previous chapter, I discussed how knowing the pulse of your town will help to put you in the right places at the right times, thus maximizing your fare potential. In this chapter, I will discuss some of the hiccups of the system, frustrations, and things to look out for as a driver—and remedies for these situations.

DRIVING PROFITS AND MAKING BANK

Wrong Pin Drops

A very common occurrence you'll find as a driver is the "Wrong Pin Drop." This is where either the rider inputs the wrong pickup location or the app glitches and displays an incorrect pickup location.

Rider initiated Wrong Pin Drops can be the result of simple human error or the slightly more malicious act of a rider purposely dropping a pin outside of a Surge Zone and then contacting you with the actual pickup location.

Over time, I've had several aggravating instances of accepting a request, driving to the pickup location, finding no passenger there, and, upon making contact with the rider, having him or her say, "I'm at _____," which in many cases, was nowhere *near* the pickup point the rider put into the app!

A good habit to get into is to text your rider after accepting a ride request asking him or her to confirm the pickup location. "Hi, ____. This your driver, _____, confirming your pickup at _____. I should be there in about ____ minutes." If the pickup location is wrong, you have the discretion to pick the person up at the actual pickup point, to cancel the request (no show or wrong destination), or to ask the person to cancel and request another ride.

HICCUPS OF THE SYSTEM

Unclear Pin Drops

Related but slightly different from the "Wrong Pin Drop" is the "Unclear Pin Drop," which often gives you a pickup address along the lines of "1029–1039 Main Street," as opposed to a definite address of "1033 Main Street" or "Main Street Bar (1033 Main Street)."

Pickup points that come in as address ranges are usually the result of riders dragging their pins on the map or the GPS defaulting to a map location as opposed to riders entering a definitive address in the app. These errors can cause you to end up a block or more away from the actual pickup location.

In the past, I have allowed the GPS to guide me to the estimated pickup point only to arrive and find no rider in the area. Upon making contact, I'd learn the rider could be a block away on the next street or even several blocks away, nowhere near the pickup point!

Should you arrive at a pickup point and no rider is there, try to make contact. If a passenger does not come out after five minutes, you are eligible to collect a no show fee, provided you attempted to make contact with the person.

To prevent the hassle of going to a wrong pickup point, though, a best practice in cases where the pickup point is unclear is to call the rider or send a text requesting confirmation and clarification.

"Hi, ____. This is your driver, _____. I am on my way to pick you up. Can you confirm your pickup address and location? It was unclear on the app."

Far Distance Pickups

Occasionally, you will get ride requests that are over thirty minutes away from you. This situation is especially common on Lyft. Most long Lyft requests are about thirty minutes away. Occasionally, I've received requests forty-five minutes away. Uber requests, at most, are twenty minutes away.

Economically speaking, accepting a ride request farther than thirty minutes away does not make financial sense unless you're already in a slow area with little activity going on and need a relocation anyway. The rideshare companies frown upon not accepting requests, and in the past, they used acceptance rates as a determining factor in deactivating driver partners. Due to recent court rulings, they can no longer hold acceptance rates against you, but they will "highly encourage" you through emails and texts to accept all ride requests.

A best practice strategy when receiving a long distance pickup request is to call the rider and ask where he needs to go.

If the ride is long, it's probably okay to accept it. If it's a short ride, you can advise him it's not feasible for you (unless you negotiate a generous tip in advance), and ask him to cancel the request and re-request the ride since a closer driver may then be available. Most passengers will cooperate and cancel right away. Some passengers won't, so you'll either need to cancel the request yourself or play a "cancel waiting game" with them. In those situations, you can either just drive on the other rideshare company's platform (for example, if the request came in on Lyft, switch to driving for Uber until the rider cancels the Lyft request) or cancel the request on your end, which, however, could affect your acceptance rating.

Canceled Rides

Probably the most aggravating hiccup of the system is the "canceled ride" request. Few things will irk you more as a driver than accepting a ride request, starting to drive to the pickup point, and a few minutes into the ride, receiving a "rider has canceled the request" message!

While irritating, these are relatively minor if only a minute or so has elapsed. The absolutely aggravating cancellations come when you're within a minute or a block of the pickup point and the rider decides to cancel on you!

DRIVING PROFITS AND MAKING BANK

Again, as a best practice, it's good simply to text the rider upon accepting the request to let her know you're on your way and should be there in a few minutes.

"Hi, _____! This is ____, your driver. I'm on my way to you at _____ and should be there in a few minutes. See you soon!"

Most riders will text back and acknowledge they'll be waiting. Some riders may not reply; those are usually the concerning ones who may wind up either cancelling on you or being no shows.

This situation is rare, but there are some inconsiderate riders who will request a ride on both Uber and Lyft at the same time and then take a ride with the first driver to show up, canceling on the other. Not cool at all.

No Show Riders

One of the more aggravating aspects of driving, as with anything else in life, is being stood up by a rider. You accept a request, drive to the pickup point, arrive, and wait...and wait...and wait. You've been stood up! You try to contact the rider and get no answer. It sucks, but it's not a total loss. If you wait for the five-minute grace period to elapse and attempt to contact the rider via text or phone, you can cancel the ride and collect a no show fee.

Provided it was a short ride anyway, the no show fee is often on par with ride fees you'd collect for a completed ride.

One thing to note is to be aware of your pickup areas. If the pickup point is in a high traffic area with no stopping or standing signs, you'll need to move to another area to wait out the five minutes before cancelling. Always be aware of traffic signs and laws!

I once had a no show outside of a popular bar. I didn't notice the no waiting sign. A cop pulled up behind me, gave me a warning, and asked me to move on. I'm glad he was gracious and didn't cite me, but I could've potentially missed the ride and caught the ticket. The no show fee would not have been worth that hassle!

Quirky GPS

A final "hiccup" of the system is the wonky nature of GPS. GPS for the most part gets you where you need to go in the most efficient way possible.

Having said that, though, sometimes GPS fails!

Below are some of the ways GPS has failed and displayed its wonkiness during my time as a driver.

DRIVING PROFITS AND MAKING BANK

Sometimes, it takes you to the back of a property. When doing pickup or drop off requests at one of the major hotels in my area, the GPS always routed me to the loading dock in the back of the hotel for whatever odd reason! I'd be arriving at the pick-up point thinking that's where the riders were, but it would turn out they were in the lobby in the front of the hotel (like most normal people), so I'd need to circle the block and figure out where the lobby was.

On several occasions when I had to pick up at an apartment building, the GPS would take me to the back of the building, so the passengers would need to hike to the back to get to me.

Sometimes, the GPS has just plain taken me to the wrong place. On one occasion, I was going to pick up a carload of girls. The GPS took me a half mile down the road from the actual address. I spent several minutes driving up and down the street in the middle of the night looking for them.

Finally, sometimes the GPS gives you a very strange route. In my town, for some reason, when navigating to the airport, the GPS routes you *past* the airport and back around through back roads. Needless to say, I no longer pay any attention to my GPS when heading to the airport.

HICCUPS OF THE SYSTEM

Summary

Life as a driver includes dealing with all the *hiccups* of the system. Some of the common things you'll need to learn and get used to dealing with include wrong pin drops, unclear pin drops, distant pickup requests, canceled rides, rider no shows, and the quirks of GPS. Texting your riders to confirm pickup locations can help to alleviate mishaps caused by incorrect and unclear pins and lessen your chance of being canceled on or having a no show. In cases of long distance pickup requests, call your rider for more information on trip destination to help decide whether it's worth your time to make the trip.

Driving Forward

Get ready to take to the road! It's a best practice to contact and confirm requests and pickup locations with your passengers via text and occasionally by phone. Let's work on developing a quick boilerplate message you can save and use when contacting passengers.

1. Write out and save a boiler plate text message you can send to ride requesters confirming pickup location once you've accepted them.

2. Script out a quick phone message you can use when calling long distance pickup ride requests.

CHAPTER 14
WHEN NATURE CALLS

"How long a minute is depends on which side
of the bathroom door you're on."

— Zall's Second Law

The Rearview Mirror

In the last chapter, I talked about the hiccups of the rideshare system, including wrong and unclear pin drops, far distance ride pickups, canceled ride requests, no shows, and quirky GPS issues. In this chapter, I will take a look at dealing with a far more basic human issue—what to do when nature calls!

DRIVING PROFITS AND MAKING BANK

Nature Calls

Let's face it—we are all answerable to the call of nature! When you need to go, you need to go. And when you're stuck in traffic and need to go, it makes things way more interesting. It's not like you've got the comfort and convenience of an office building with a restroom just a few steps down the hall. You're sitting in traffic, need to drop off someone, and then drive to the nearest publicly-accessible restroom! If you're in a traffic jam, you're in for a world of hurt. In this chapter, we'll spend some time talking about tips for surviving nature's call on the road.

Finding a Facility

The Most Accessible Facilities

When it comes to restrooms in public areas, you'll basically have the following options, all of which should be relatively near to you:

- Shopping Malls, Strip Malls, Shopping Centers
- Restaurants
- Gas Stations
- Public Parks

Malls

Malls are a great choice since just about every community has a shopping center or strip mall, and most towns have a shopping mall. A good portion of your drop offs will be at shopping centers or malls, so I always take time for a bathroom break if I get a drop off at one of these locations. Generally speaking, mall restaurant bathrooms are fairly clean and well-kept.

Most shopping malls will have open restrooms. Many strip malls or shopping centers may require a key code to enter.

Restaurants

Another great pick for a bathroom break is a restaurant. Typically, fast food places have the most accessible restrooms since you don't need to deal with host staff. Fast food restaurants are conveniently located just about everywhere, so you can quickly pull in, do your business, and get a quick snack, meal, or drink before getting back on the road. Restaurant restroom facilities are also fairly well-kept and clean. Many restaurants bathrooms now require a key code to enter.

Gas Stations

Gas stations are also conveniently located everywhere. If it's time to refuel, get a snack, or a cold drink, you can always pull over, do your business, and refuel your car and body. Gas station restroom facility cleanliness may not always be a priority. Many gas station restrooms require a key code.

Public Parks

Public parks are available in every community. These restrooms are just about always open entry, requiring no key codes, but the cleanliness scale may leave *a lot* to be desired.

Key Codes

Given that many restrooms in shopping centers, restaurants, and gas stations require a key code, one thing that may help is to keep a note file on your smartphone listing the restrooms you frequent and their respective key codes. You can update this file regularly as you find more restrooms and as codes change. I personally recommend Evernote for this, but even something like a Google Sheets file or the default notepad app that came with your phone will suffice.

WHEN NATURE CALLS

Summary

In this chapter, we took a quick look at restroom facilities that are easily accessible and available to you should you need to answer nature's call out on the road. Shopping malls, fast food restaurants, gas stations, and public parks are in every neighborhood and town, and they are fairly accessible, although many require a key code. Facilities that also sell food and drinks are enticing locations for answering nature's call.

Driving Forward

Get ready to get out on the road and answer nature's call! Make a list of malls, restaurants, gas stations, or parks in each area of your town you're aware of and comfortable with visiting to do your business.

1. Make a list of the different parts of your town.

2. In each part of town, note five shopping malls, restaurants, coffee shops, gas stations, etc. where you can use restroom facilities. Build upon and revise this list over time, noting bathroom codes, if any.

PART III
NOT A JOB, A BUSINESS

CHAPTER 15

INDEPENDENT CONTRACTOR STATUS

"Entrepreneurship is not a part-time job, and it's not even a full-time job. It's a lifestyle."

— Carrie Layne

The Rearview Mirror

In the previous sections of this book, I talked about what rideshare driving is and gave you a glimpse into the day-to-day life of a rideshare driver and what you can expect. In this and the next few chapters, I'll delve into small business basics. Rideshare driving is not a "job" in the traditional sense. Rideshare driving sets you up as a small business owner, and along with that come many responsibilities most of us are not trained for.

Independent Contractor Status

One of the distinguishing things about being a rideshare driver is that you are *not* an employee of Uber or Lyft or any other ride-share company you belong to (unless it's classified you as such). Rideshare drivers are independent contractors of the rideshare companies. Much like if you are in the direct sales or multi-level marketing industries with companies like DoTerra, Young Living, Arbonne, Avon, Amway, Pampered Chef, Mary Kay, Jamberry, Body by Vi, or Nerium, you are *not* an employee of the company but rather an "Independent Consultant," "Independent Distributor," or "Independent Marketing Executive." In the rideshare industry, you are referred to as a "Driver Partner." All of these terms mean one thing, ultimately: In the eyes of the IRS, you are an independent contractor and thus a small business owner or a 1099 worker, as opposed to a W-2 worker (wage employee).

As a small business owner and independent contractor, there are many things you need to be aware of and that you are re-sponsible for. If you've never done independent contract work before, you need to be aware of your responsibilities and your rights. We'll spend some time going over these in the next few sections.

Not an Employee

One of the biggest differentiations between being a 1099 independent contractor instead of a W-2 employee is that you are *not* on a salary or payroll with the company you are contracting with.

As an independent contractor, you are also not subject to a set schedule. Employers determine the when, where, what, and how of how you conduct your work. As independent contractors, typically only the *what* is defined. The *when, where,* and *how* are often your choice. Rideshare attracts people from all over because of the flexibility of schedule (the when). Time independence is part of the litmus test indicating you are not an employee and allowing rideshare companies to classify drivers as independent contractors.

As an independent contractor and driver partner, you are also not subject to a defined workload. There are no penalties if you only drive once a week. You have the freedom to drive as often, or as infrequently, as you wish. Control of your own workload is another element in the litmus test that rideshare companies use to identify you as an independent contractor.

DRIVING PROFITS AND MAKING BANK

On the downside, as an independent contractor, you do not have the right to benefits typically associated with employment.

No Benefits

Most people working for a wage also seek the Holy Trinity of benefits—health insurance, retirement accounts, and paid time off. Make no mistake, those are *all* very desirable and good to have if you're seeking a regular job—anyone would tell you to work for employers who offer all of those in spades! (Government jobs are typically the best for that.)

When you are self-employed, *you* are responsible for providing all of that for yourself. As an independent contractor partnering with Uber or Lyft, the rideshare company does not owe you any of those benefits. If you were an employee of the company, then by law, it would owe you many of those things if you reached certain thresholds of hours worked. This is the most controversial area of Uber and Lyft's business model and labor practices—and it has been, and continues to be, contested in courts nationwide. This is not limited to just Uber and Lyft. Many companies in the "gig" and "sharing economy" face these same troubles, whether you deliver groceries on Instacart, Postmates, or DoorDash, or you do handiwork around the house as a TaskRabbit or on Handy.

INDEPENDENT CONTRACTOR STATUS

With medical costs soaring, and people's nest eggs shrinking, future health and retirement benefits are crucially important, so it is understandable that gig economy workers everywhere are looking to get that crucial piece of the pie.

What many gig economy, independent consultants, or small business owners *don't* realize, however, is that it is relatively easy to set up both health and retirement benefits for yourself. Funding the accounts is much trickier, but setting them up is easy. I will explain this process in Chapter 17.

Paying Taxes

The final consideration we will look at here is that as a small business owner/independent contractor/driver partner, you are required to pay federal and state income taxes, and depending on your jurisdiction, local taxes as well.

As W-2 wage earners, we are used to having our employers withhold taxes and prepay them to the government for us, ensuring we don't run into tax trouble at the end of the year.

As an independent contractor, the burden is on *you* to figure out how much you owe and to *set aside* part of your earnings to pay your taxes. This is easier said than done given the flexible nature of self-employment earnings. Still, it is incumbent upon you to endeavor to take all your earnings, set aside a certain amount (best practice says about 30 percent), and send in tax payments each quarter.

While I am not a tax professional, I do cover some basic tax tips in Chapter 19. You are, of course, advised to seek the guidance of, and work with, a licensed or qualified tax professional, such as a CPA or tax attorney.

Summary

In this chapter, I provided a general rundown of the differences between being an employee (W-2 earner) and an Independent Contractor (1099 earner). Independent contractors, by definition, are small business owners and have freedom of choice over work conditions. As non-employees, they are not entitled to traditional benefits like health insurance, retirement benefits, or paid leave, and they are expected to provision for their own health and retirement. Finally, independent contractors need to be aware that they are responsible for withholding and paying their own taxes at regular intervals.

Driving Forward

Let's talk about employment benefits as you plan and develop your ridesharing business.

1. Do you plan to drive in addition to holding a regular job, or will you drive full-time?

2. Will you have medical coverage if you drive (from your regular job, spouse, etc.), or will you need to find medical coverage on your own?

3. Do you have retirement benefits through an employer? If not, would you be interested in setting up retirement benefits for yourself through your business earnings?

CHAPTER 16

BUSINESS REGISTRATION, ENTITIES, AND BANK ACCOUNTS

"You know that if you can make a business get off the ground, then you are absolutely capable of accomplishing anything in this world."

— Kristen Prescott

The Rearview Mirror

In the last chapter, I discussed the differences between independent contractors (1099 workers) and employees (W-2 workers) and the various rights, benefits, and responsibilities each has. In this chapter, I will discuss business registration requirements, trade names, trademarks, service marks, the different business entity types, and setting up banking and insurance requirements.

Business Registration and Licensing

Business registrations and licensing requirements vary by jurisdiction since laws may vary state by state or city by city.

Typically, to register a business so it is legally recognized as one, you will file paperwork with your state's "Department of Business" or "Department of Commerce"—whatever it may be called where you are.

Depending on the type of business you are registering and how heavily regulated your industry is, you may also be required to file additional forms or apply for licenses or certifications. Examples include health licenses if you operate a food service or restaurant, medical or dental licenses if you are a practicing physician, etc. The taxi industry has long been regulated, so its drivers are required to be licensed as taxi drivers in most jurisdictions. Since rideshare is still a new industry, many local governments are still determining how best to regulate it. Uber and

Lyft's city pages for your city will have information on all current government requirements to register. You can also always call or contact your state's department of business or commerce for all requirements to register your rideshare business.

Business Entities

When registering your business, you will need to choose a business entity type. There are five basic business entity types:

1. Sole Proprietorships
2. Partnerships
3. Limited Liability Companies (LLCs)
4. S Corporations
5. Corporations

I will now define and share the advantages and disadvantages of each.

Sole Proprietorship

A sole proprietorship is the most basic form of business. Unless you've registered your business otherwise, your business is by default a sole proprietorship.

As such, a sole proprietorship is the easiest and least burdensome type of business to set up.

On the downside, a sole proprietorship leaves you the most open to personal liability. In the eyes of the law, in a sole proprietorship, there is no distinction between the business owner and the business itself; both are one and the same. As such, any business debts or liabilities also become the owner's personal debts and liabilities.

Most business consultants (including myself) or legal professionals would advise most business owners not to register their business as a sole proprietorship due to the strain of personal liability you would incur should the business fail financially or incur other types of liability. Some of the other business entity types we will cover provide a separation of personal and business assets, sheltering you as the owner from some of your business' liabilities.

Partnership

A partnership functions similarly to a sole proprietorship with the difference being that the business has multiple owners. Due to the nature of partnerships, they are slightly more difficult to form than a sole proprietorship since the partners will need to draft a partnership agreement to serve as the business's governing document. Like a sole proprietorship, partners in the business do assume personal risk for any business debts or liabilities.

LLC

A Limited Liability Company (LLC) offers a layer of protection for business owners. For legal purposes, the business LLC is a separate legal entity from the owner. As such, you, the business owner, have some level of insulation and protection of your personal assets from any debts or liabilities your business incurs. In an LLC, the business owner(s) is/are referred to as "Members." An LLC can have a single-member or multiple members. As such, the LLC is the most flexible business entity, combining the ease and flexibility of set-up as sole proprietorships or partnerships with many of the protective traits of a corporation. When registering an LLC, you need to file an "Articles of Organization" and an "Operating Agreement." Most state registration forms for an LLC business are basically the Articles of Organization form. The "Operating Agreement" is comparable to the "Partnership Agreement," which serves as the governing document for the business, detailing how the business will be run, how profits and losses are allocated, how members can join or leave the company, and whatever other details are needed. If you are a single-member LLC, the Operating Agreement is relatively easy to draft because there are no other partners or members with whom to hash things out. For tax purposes, all profits or losses from an LLC "pass through" to the members and are claimed on Schedule C of your tax return. This is different from the traditional corporation, which subjects the business and the owner to double taxation. In an LLC, only the owner is taxed, not the business itself.

S Corporations and Corporations

The last two types of business entities I will talk about are S Corporations and Corporations. While they are two separate types of business entities, I will address them together due to their similarities.

A Corporation (also known as a C Corporation) is what most of us think of when we hear the term business. Corporations use the "Inc." suffix on the business name to note that they are "incorporated." As a business entity, the business corporation is a separate legal entity from its owner. The owners of a corporation are known as "shareholders," each of whom owns a certain amount of stock in the company. Corporations offer the greatest amount of insulation of personal assets from business debts and liabilities because of the nature of the business laws surrounding corporations given they are separate and distinct legal entities from their owners/shareholders.

While corporations do offer the most protection for owners, they are also the most burdensome to operate due to all the legal requirements surrounding them. A board of directors must be formed and meet regularly. This board has legal oversight over the company and is ultimately responsible for its operations and compliance with the law. Regular meetings of all company shareholders must also be held. An annual report of the company's operations must be filed with the appropriate government authority.

All of this oversight is offered in exchange for the extraordinary protections that corporations offer business owners in terms of limiting personal liability. Another feature and disadvantage of the corporation model is the double taxation to which shareholders are exposed. The corporation itself is taxed by the government, and any earnings made by shareholders either as corporate salary or as investment dividends are taxable income as well.

S Corporations have the same requirements and advantages as C Corporations. The difference between them is taxation. S Corporations offer the same pass-through taxation as LLCs, where any business earnings are claimed on the Schedule K-1 on your tax form. There is no double taxation. The business entity itself is not taxed—only the shareholders are.

Recommendations

The overhead of operating a corporation is typically too burdensome for most business owners unless they are truly seeking to limit their liabilities. For the average business owner, most consultants or advisors would advise against registering as a corporation.

Because of the liability you open yourself up to as a sole proprietor, most advisors would recommend against registering as a sole proprietorship.

For the purposes of your rideshare business, you most likely will want to register as an LLC. Given your personal tax situation, registering as an S Corporation may also be a viable option given it further limits your liability while offering the same pass-through taxation benefits of an LLC. The extra burden of record keeping may not be worth it. It is best to talk with your tax advisor or a good business attorney to figure out what is the best way for you to register your rideshare business.

Tradenames, Trademarks, Service Marks

Tradenames

When registering your business, you'll also want to consider registering a "trade name" for your business. Trade names are basically the names we know most businesses by. As an example, you may have formally chosen to register your business as "Chad's Driving Service, LLC," or "Tony's Awesome Rideshare, Inc." Later, however, you decide those names are difficult to market under so you decide to market your service under the name "San Antonio Safe Rides," or "San Antonio Safe Transportation and Tours." In this case, you will want to register "San Antonio Safe Rides" or "San Antonio Safe Transportation and Tours" as the trade name under which your business operates. Often, you'll see trade names noted alongside the actual business name as in "Chad's Driving Service, LLC dba (doing business as) San Antonio Safe Rides."

Registering your trade name with your city, county, state, or federal business authority protects your business name from appropriation and use by other businesses, thus reducing any potential marketplace confusion.

Trademarks

Trademarks are similar to trade names, but they specifically reference the brand identity you've developed for your products, allowing you to differentiate your products from those of your competitors. Typically, this trademark will refer to your business logo or names you've developed for specific products you sell. For example, your company logo can be trademarked.

Service Marks

Service marks are basically the same as a trademark, but they refer to the identity you've developed for a service you provide (as opposed to a product). In the case of your rideshare business, you would be registering a service mark, not a trademark. If you have a company logo for "San Antonio Safe Rides," you can register that as a service mark. If you offer a service for driving the elderly in San Antonio that you call "San Antonio Safe Elder Rides," or a service for late night rides called "San Antonio Rides After Dark," you could register service marks for each.

Business Banking

When running a business, it is best to keep your business banking separate from your personal banking. It simplifies the accounting process. If you are setting up as an LLC, S Corporation, or C Corporation, you are required by law to keep your business and personal finances separate.

When opening your business bank accounts, you will need to provide your business documents such as articles of incorporation, articles of organization, an operating agreement, and/or bylaws.

Insurance

As a business owner, you typically will want to carry some type of business liability insurance to protect and shield you in the event something bad happens. Uber and Lyft do both provide insurance coverage for you through their policies when you are en route to your passengers and when you are driving them to their final destinations. However, there are still insurance "gaps" that are unaccounted for. Many jurisdictions continue to pass laws requiring extra insurance coverage such as for rideshare insurance riders in your personal policy or commercial driver's insurance to close these insurance gaps. For rideshare drivers, laws are still being written and developed in various jurisdictions. You will want to check the Uber and Lyft city pages for where you live to get the latest information. As a best practice, though, because it is a driving job, you may want to consider looking into commercial driver insurance for full protection. These policies may be cost-prohibitive if you are only driving part-time, but for full-time drivers, they may be worth considering, especially if you are looking at adding a spin-off business such as private tours. (I will discuss building other businesses in Chapter 26.)

Summary

In this chapter, I discussed business registrations, entities, and basic intellectual property protection. I recommend that you seek the advice of, and work with, a qualified legal professional in your jurisdiction. Business registrations can be done with the appropriate state or local government authority in your jurisdiction. You will more than likely want to register your rideshare business as an LLC, or possibly as an S Corporation. Again, you will want to consult with a qualified business attorney or tax professional to help weigh the benefits for your specific situation. In registering your business, you will need to create the appropriate business documents, such as articles of incorporation, articles of organization, and operating agreements. Templates are available online, or you can work with a qualified business attorney. Local laws may require you to carry additional insurance.

Driving Forward

Let's get you ready to give birth to your rideshare business by initiating the registration process.

1. Research the process of starting a business in your state and city, and identify which government agencies you will need to contact to do so.

2. Name your rideshare business and register it under that name, *or* register the appropriate trade name for it.

3. Find templates to draft the documents you need to form an LLC in your state and city (articles of organization, operating agreement).

4. Research the insurance requirements for rideshare drivers in your state, and start looking for a good insurance plan.

CHAPTER 17

HEALTH AND RETIREMENT BENEFITS

"Take care of your body. It's the only place you have to live."

— Jim Rohn

The Rearview Mirror

In the last chapter, I discussed how to register your business, protect some of your brand and intellectual property from market confusion, and the different types of business entities under which you can form your business. In this chapter, I will revisit the self-employment health and retirement benefits we touched on in Chapter 15.

DRIVING PROFITS AND MAKING BANK

Benefits for the Self-Employed

As you may recall from Chapter 15, I talked about how as a self-employed worker you are responsible for funding any traditional work benefits you want or need, such as health and retirement benefits. As an independent contractor, you do not have an employer to provide and help fund those things for you—you are on your own. In the next few sections, I will discuss benefit resources you can use to cover this gap.

Health Benefits

While neither Uber nor Lyft directly provides health insurance, both have partnered with companies that specialize in helping self-employed, gig economy workers get the health insurance they need. Uber partners with Stride Health, while Lyft partners with eHealth. Both companies specialize in helping gig economy and self-employed online business owners acquire health insurance.

A final option, if you are on your own acquiring health insurance, is to go to the government health insurance marketplace established by the Affordable Care Act (commonly known as Obamacare) at healthcare.gov. Under the Affordable Care Act, government health exchanges make finding health coverage easier for Americans because providers are not allowed to discriminate due to things like preexisting conditions. If you are low income, government assistance is available to ensure that you can afford and acquire coverage. Health insurance is something all Americans have access to. While traditional, employer-provided health coverage may provide comprehensive coverage to most Americans, the government-supported plans through the marketplace do provide access to those otherwise unable to acquire coverage. For workers with Uber, Lyft, other gig economy jobs, and online companies, Stride Health and eHealth assist in connecting workers with the right insurance coverage for their needs.

Of course, if you are married or young and eligible for coverage under your spouse or parents' plan, that coverage is still your best bet.

Retirement Benefits

Those with employer-provided retirement programs are used to having a pension, 401(k), 403(b), or 457(b) that they or their employer contribute to. For those of us with the means to do so, we also set-up IRA accounts to contribute to in order to secure our future and golden years. When you are self-employed, *you* are the employer responsible for setting up all of these accounts and contributing to them, provided you earn enough to do so.

When you are self-employed, you are eligible for any of the retirement programs below:

- Simplified Employee Pension (SEP-IRA)

- Solo 401(k)

- SIMPLE IRA

I encourage you to consult a qualified professional financial advisor or financial planner to explore your options and set up your self-employed retirement accounts. Individuals holding credentials such as Certified Financial Planner, Chartered Financial Analyst, Chartered Financial Consultant, and Chartered Alternative Investment Analyst typically have the education and experience to advise you competently and are worthy of your trust and confidence.

Summary

In this chapter, I discussed how you can set up your own health and retirement benefits if you are looking to do rideshare driving full-time and do not have any other source of health or retirement benefits. Uber and Lyft partner with companies (Stride and eHealth) that help self-employed, gig economy workers acquire health benefits. The government health insurance marketplace is the one stop source for all Americans to find health coverage. In regards to retirement benefits, self-employed workers can set up different plans such as a SEP IRA, Solo 401(k), or SIMPLE IRA for their retirements. In setting up your retirement, you should work with a qualified financial professional to help you go over options and set up plans.

Driving Forward

Let's secure your financial future if you are looking to be self-employed full-time as a driver and/or want to sock away more into retirement accounts by ensuring you have health coverage and retirement benefits.

- If you are in need of health insurance coverage and you are a qualifying driver, visit Strider Health (Uber), eHealth (Lyft), and healthcare.gov on the web.

- Consult your financial advisor (or find one) to inquire about setting up a solo 401(k) or SEP IRA.

CHAPTER 18
ACCOUNTING

"The only way to get out of the 'Rat Race' is to prove your proficiency at both accounting and investing, arguably two of the most difficult subjects to master."

— Robert Kiyosaki

The Rearview Mirror

In the last chapter, I discussed how you can set up health and retirement benefits for yourself as a self-employed worker. In this chapter, I will discuss the day-to-day accounting and tracking requirements of running your business and how to maximize your profits and optimize your tax savings.

DRIVING PROFITS AND MAKING BANK

Bookkeeping

Bookkeeping is an important part of being a business owner. Bookkeeping helps you to determine whether or not your business is making money. It can help you to determine and control costs (trim the fat), thereby increasing your profits. Ultimately, bookkeeping is also an important part of meeting government regulations, such as filing and paying your taxes.

The basics of bookkeeping are the same for all business types, or even for your own personal household. You need to track your expenses (all of your spending) and your income (all the money you are bringing in). As a business owner, you want to keep all your purchase receipts and copies of all your invoices. For rideshare, this is relatively easy because the app provides you with all your income receipts and keeps records of earnings longitudinally. For expenses, though, you will want to keep copies of everything, such as gas receipts, repair and maintenance receipts, car washes, insurance payments, and/or car payments. All are legitimate business expenses and deductible from your taxes.

When doing your bookkeeping, you will want to use good bookkeeping software such as QuickBooks Self-Employed (downloadable and usable both as a phone app and on the web) or work with a qualified certified public accountant.

Mileage Tracking

Another consideration when it comes to accounting for rideshare driving is keeping track of your driving mileage. When doing your taxes, you can deduct rideshare driving mileage expenses as a business expense either by taking the standard deduction or submitting your documentation for mileage, if it is beyond the standard deduction.

With rideshare driving, both Uber and Lyft provide a report of the miles you drove while on each ride with a passenger, which helps you track your miles. However, Uber and Lyft do not track the miles you drove to a pickup, which can double the mileage for many rides.

You can use two basic methods to track your miles:

1. **Good old pen and paper:** You can keep some type of notebook and note your odometer reading when you start your rideshare shift and then note the odometer reading when you end the shift, and then do the math yourself.

2. **Use an app:** Many apps exist that you can download to your phone. Each app will then will use its GPS to track your routes and miles, allowing you to classify all your trips as either business or personal.

Some of the popular mileage apps you can look into include:

- Sherapshare
- Stride Drive
- Hurdlr
- MileIQ
- Triplog

QuickBooks Self-Employed also includes a mileage tracking feature in its app. Because of its comprehensive bookkeeping and mileage tracking features, it is what I personally use for my business accounting needs.

Professional Accountant

When keeping your books, it's a good idea to work with a qualified CPA either to audit or assist in your bookkeeping. Software programs such as QuickBooks are very powerful tools that provide great guidance in optimizing your deductions, but there's nothing like working with a trusted advisor who knows your personal situation—someone you can get on the phone or drop by and talk to when needed.

You can ask for referrals from family or friends or use online tools such as AccountantsWorld.com or Yelp to find an accountant near you.

Summary

In this chapter, I discussed bookkeeping, both for practical purposes, such as knowing how much your business is making, to more regulatory and legal purposes, such as being organized for paying your taxes. I also discussed tracking your driving miles as a tax deduction. I shared some handy apps you can use for both accounting and mileage tracking. Finally, I discussed finding a good accountant who can assist with your bookkeeping.

Driving Forward

Let's get you prepared and squared away to keep your business accounting.

1. Get referrals for a good accountant if you do not have one already.

2. Check out QuickBooks Self-Employed.

3. Read reviews on and test out the recommended mileage tracking apps.

CHAPTER 19
PAYING YOUR TAXES

"In this world nothing can be said to be certain
except death and taxes."

— Benjamin Franklin

The Rearview Mirror

In the last chapter, I discussed the importance of bookkeeping when running your business. In this chapter, I will discuss that all important topic of taxes. A friendly reminder and disclaimer: *I am not a qualified tax professional* but rather a business consultant who is providing generalized information. *You should seek the advice of and work with a qualified tax professional, such as a tax attorney or tax CPA, to find solutions specific to your individual situation.*

DRIVING PROFITS AND MAKING BANK

Taxes When Self-Employed

Everyone pays taxes no matter his or her walk of life. When you are self-employed, the tax burden in particular is trickier and greater. As mentioned in Chapter 15, self-employed people have extra responsibilities when it comes to taxes because they do not have employers withholding and paying their taxes. Instead, if you are self-employed, you are responsible for withholding and paying your own taxes.

When it comes to self-employment, there are three types of taxes we need to be mindful of:

1. Federal and State Income Taxes

2. Self-Employment Taxes (FICA)

3. Local and Business Taxes or Fees (Sales, Excise, Other)

Federal and state income taxes are a percentage of our earnings. As an employee, our employer would be responsible for withholding these taxes and paying them to the state or federal government. Then, every year, we file a tax return to reconcile what we owed with what we paid. As self-employed people, we still need to pay this tax and file this return, but the difference is we do not have an employer to withhold any earnings, so we need to calculate what we owe at least every quarter and make a tax payment. This is complicated by the government's quarters not being every three months. The "quarters" are really three months, two, three, and then four months. Compounding this is the tricky question of whether we've even made any money with our business to have income to withhold.

Self-employment taxes are taxes self-employed people pay to fund their FICA, Social Security, and Medicare. As with federal and state income tax, these are usually withheld from your paycheck. When you're self-employed, however, you are responsible for determining what you owe and paying the appropriate tax. Again, this is complicated when, as a self-employed worker, you are uncertain what your income will be, if any.

Local and other business taxes are assessed at the state, city, or county level, depending on the jurisdiction you live in; they include sales taxes, excise taxes, or other fees charged for any number of reasons in your local jurisdiction. Your local commerce or business department will typically send reminders or forms to fill in to your registered business or email addresses before due dates.

Set Up Payroll

In taking care of your business taxes, you can do two basic things:

1. Work with a qualified tax professional such as an accountant or tax attorney.

2. Use a software accounting and payroll system such as QuickBooks.

When you are self-employed, typically, the government will want you to pay what's called "Estimated Taxes" each quarter. As the name implies, you estimate your earnings based on your records and projections, and you send quarterly payments based on your estimates. This process can be and does get tricky because the nature of self-employment makes estimating very difficult. Nevertheless, the taxes must be paid.

If you need assistance doing estimates, you can work with your accountant to run calculations and determine what your estimated income and taxes are, and submit the appropriate forms and payments when they are due.

Conversely, if you are using accounting software such as QuickBooks, it will also help you estimate your taxes, file and send in the appropriate forms, and transmit the payments for you.

Another strategy you can follow is to set up a payroll system for yourself whereby you draw a regular paycheck from your company (your LLC or S Corporation is your employer) and taxes are withheld and sent off as if you were employed by any other company.

Work with an Accountant and a Tax Advisor

Regardless of how you choose to take care of your taxes, it is *always* a good idea to work with a qualified tax professional, such as a tax attorney or a tax CPA, to ensure you are in compliance with all laws. I will go over tips on how to find a qualified professional to work with in Chapter 20.

Summary

In this chapter, I discussed paying your taxes as a business owner. As a self-employed worker, you are responsible for deducting and paying taxes on your earnings. To calculate and file your taxes, you can either work with a qualified tax CPA or use accounting software such as QuickBooks to calculate your estimated taxes, and then file and pay them at the regular due date intervals.

Driving Forward

Let's get you into compliance with paying your taxes!

1. Meet with your qualified tax professional to discuss tax strategies and accounting for your situation given your new rideshare venture.

2. Download and set up QuickBooks or any bookkeeping and tax software of your choice.

CHAPTER 20
PROFESSIONAL ADVICE

"Leave it to the professionals."

— Adage

The Rearview Mirror

In the previous chapter, I discussed strategies to estimate and pay your taxes as a self-employed worker. In this chapter, I will share strategies on finding the professional assistance you need to keep your business and life running smoothly. Specifically, I'll help you start down the path to finding a good accountant, financial planner, and attorney you can count on to keep you compliant, in the black, and watch your back during any hard times.

DRIVING PROFITS AND MAKING BANK

General Strategies for Finding a Professional

Your Personal Network

Generally speaking, when it comes to getting any type of professional advice and assistance, you can always leverage your personal network. You may have family members, friends, classmates, or others in your extended network who are practicing accountants, financial advisors, or attorneys. If you don't know anyone in these fields personally, then your family or friends may be able to recommend someone. As a first step, you can always leverage this network.

Online Directories and Reviews

Beyond that, you can always tap into online directories and reviews to find professionals of good quality and repute. General peer and crowdsource reviews at websites like Yelp are great for more than just finding restaurants. Many industries also offer industry-specific directories with peer and crowd reviews for practitioners. Accounting, financial planning, and legal professionals are no exception.

Accountant

What to Look For

When it comes to accounting assistance, you will want to find an accountant who can assist with the following:

- Bookkeeping
- Tax preparation
- Auditing

Bookkeeping, tax preparation, and auditing are all musts for accounting services. Your accountant should also be a certified public accountant (CPA). Then you can rest assured that your accountant knows what he or she is doing with your business records and accounting.

Where to Find an Accountant

In addition to your personal network, you can also search on a directory such as AccountantsWorld.com for a list of CPAs and CPA firms nationwide, including ones near you.

Financial Planning

What to Look For

When looking for a good financial advisor or financial planner, the person you choose should be able to do the following for you and your finances:

- Set up retirement accounts
- Discuss investment strategies and evaluate investment instruments
- Discuss debt-reduction strategies
- Discuss and develop budgeting strategies
- Discuss and develop tax-optimization strategies
- Discuss and develop risk-management strategies and insurance

The professional you choose should hold a Certified Financial Planner (CFP), Chartered Financial Consultant (ChFC), or similar credential.

Where to Find a Financial Planner

In addition to your personal network, you can also search online directories such as LetsMakeAPlan.org or NAPFA.org for a qualified professional.

Your local banks, local branches of major investment firms, or other local financial advising companies will all have local listings if you wish to go that route.

Legal

What to Look For

When it comes to the rideshare business, the attorney you choose to retain or work with should be able to provide the following services at a minimum:

- Defend you against traffic infractions
- Advocate for you in the event of an auto accident
- Advise you on tax laws related to your rideshare business
- Advise you on business laws related to your rideshare business

As a rideshare driver, you will be dealing with traffic citations and auto accidents at some point. Being out on the road constantly opens you up to greater risk for those. In the first year I drove, I had more traffic citations and auto accidents than I had had in the twenty years prior. The odds of being cited or getting into an accident go way up when you're a rideshare driver.

As a business owner, you will also need the occasional consultation on taxes or business laws for your jurisdiction.

Another possible area you'll want to consider is a good labor attorney who is knowledgeable about 1099 vs. W-2 workers. The classification of drivers as independent contractors remains controversial, and consequently, the payouts to drivers due to lack of benefits also remains a controversial area because many believe drivers are misclassified and are owed back payments for unpaid benefits.

Where to Find an Attorney

In addition to your personal network, Martindale.com is a popular website for finding reviews on attorneys nationwide, including your local area. Another popular option is to take advantage of prepaid legal services through LegalShield, which allows you to subscribe to or select attorney services for a year. Legal consultations are available 24/7 for free, and courtroom defenses are available for free up to a select number of hours. Additional services are available on a discount basis. LegalShield Plans are available for personal legal assistance to individuals and families as well as for small businesses. The plans run as little as $200–$250 per year for individuals and families and $340–$500 per year for businesses. If you would like additional information on LegalShield, I'll be glad to provide it to you.

Summary

In this chapter, I discussed how to screen and where to find professional assistance in the areas of accounting, financial advising, and legal assistance. Personal networks can be a source for finding qualified professionals, or you can search online professional directories and review sites.

Driving Forward

Let's get you squared away with good and reputable professional accounting, financial, and legal assistance for your business.

1. Get a referral for a good accountant if you do not have one already.

2. Get a referral for a good financial advisor if you do not have one already.

3. Get a referral to a good attorney if you do not have one already or look into LegalShield.

PART IV
BOOSTING PROFITS

CHAPTER 21
IT'S OKAY TO DOUBLE DIP

"If you want to be more productive, you need to
become master of your minutes."

— Crystal Paine

The Rearview Mirror

In Part III, we covered business basics for the self-employed,
such as discussing the differences between an independent
contractor and an employee, the different types of business
entities, the forms and documents you need to file to register
your business, how to set up health and retirement benefits
for yourself as a self-employed worker, and how to keep track
of your business finances, including expenses, revenue, and

taxes. With our discussion of the basics of business covered, we now turn our attention to growing your business and helping you to maximize and drive your profits so you earn as much money as possible.

If Available, Drive for Both

One of the basic concepts of ridesharing, as with most things in life, is the maximization of your time. You want to be available to receive as many ride requests as possible from as many sources as possible. Therefore, as a start to maximizing your profits, you should be driving for both Uber and Lyft if both companies are operating in your town.

Keeping within the spirit of true independent contractor status, neither company has a "non-compete clause" that prohibits you from being a partner with both companies.

As a standard practice while driving, keep both apps on and "Go Online" on both apps to make yourself available for requests on both platforms. When you accept a ride request on one platform, go offline on the other so you do not affect your acceptance rates—and simply repeat this process over and over.

Receiving ride requests on both platforms is the major benefit of driving for both companies. As a driver, you'll find that it really helps to keep your downtime to a minimal. If it's a slow day or night on Uber, Lyft may be very busy. If it's a slow day or night on Lyft, Uber may be busier. The ultimate winner will be *you* because you'll be receiving requests from both services, allowing you to pick and choose the most lucrative rides and keep your downtime to a minimum.

Summary

As a driver, you want to maximize your time by taking as many ride requests as possible. Being a driver partner with both Uber and Lyft will allow you to receive requests through both apps, keeping you busy and your downtime to a minimum because a slow period on one app may be a busy period on the other. Neither company prevents you from being a partner with the other company. Most driver partners drive for both companies if both services are available in their towns.

Driving Forward

Boost your profits by making yourself available for as many ride requests as possible. Apply to drive for both Uber and Lyft if you have not done so already and if both services are in your city.

- Apply to drive for Uber at Uber.com. Please use referral code 7avf4qscue.

- Apply to drive for Lyft at Lyft.com. Please use referral code JONATHAN008938.

CHAPTER 22

RIDE THE SURGE AND BONUS

"It's being in the right place at the right time and taking advantage of your opportunities."

— Lee Majors

The Rearview Mirror

In the last chapter, I talked about maximizing your time and availability for ride requesls by driving for both Uber and Lyft and making yourself available for ride requests on both apps. In this chapter, we talk about boosting your profits through "Riding the Surge and Primetime" and taking advantage of driver bonus programs and opportunities.

DRIVING PROFITS AND MAKING BANK

Learn the Surge and Primetime Cycle

As a driver giving rides, you'll maximize your profits by being able to catch ride requests during Surges and Primetimes, often referred to as "Riding the Surge." As mentioned earlier, Uber and Lyft implement Surge and Primetime pricing, respectively, to get more drivers on the road during peak demand periods, helping to ensure there are enough drivers to meet rider demand. Surges are calculated and represented as multipliers of the base (1.5 x, 2.0 x, 3.0 x, 4.1 x, etc.), while Primetimes are presented as percentages (25, 100, 200 percent).

The trick to Riding the Surge is to have a good understanding of your city and its traffic demand times and locations because this demand is what triggers the Surges, as I discussed in depth in Chapter 12. If you go where and when the demand is, you set yourself up for landing a really good ride with a higher Surge or Primetime rate.

As a disclaimer, the nature of Surges and Primetimes can be unpredictable. Surges and Primetimes merely reflect rider demand. Given the high cost of Surges, riders may need a ride but not necessarily be willing to pay the "5.0" Surge or "200 percent" Primetime rates currently in place. Many riders may and do choose to wait for the Surge or Primetime to drop to a lower level before actually requesting a ride. It is completely possible for you to be sitting in the middle of a Surge area and not have a request come in at all, as many drivers will tell you to their collective dismay. It is also possible to be sitting in the middle of a Surge or Primetime area and receive a request from *outside* the area because you are, in fact, that requester's nearest driver. "Riding the Surge," therefore, is as much *luck* as it is setting yourself up to be in the right places at the right times.

Study Uber and Lyft's Charts

Because when you make money, the rideshare company makes money, both Uber and Lyft provide data on demand patterns that typically will reflect Surge and Primetime patterns. As mentioned, each week Uber and Lyft send emails or text messages noting demand times and patterns to help you identify the best times to make money. Uber will also aggressively message you during actual peak demand times as they emerge to encourage you to get on the road or let you know ahead of time about anticipated big events when rider demand is expected to be high.

As a driver looking to boost and maximize your profits, study these charts and plan to be on the road during these periods, your schedule permitting.

DRIVING PROFITS AND MAKING BANK

Surge Tracking Apps

Third party app developers have also developed apps available for the iPhone and Android that track Surges and Primetimes and share the collected data to help you better set yourself up in the right places at the right times.

The iOS has both "Surge" and "Primetime" apps developed by Duncan Cunningham, which allow you to track Surges on Uber and Primetime on Lyft, respectively.

Available on the Android is "Surge Chaser" by Michael Siedlecki. The Surge Chaser app is also available on the iOS.

All apps are free to download and use with the option to pay for premium features. Take advantage of these apps to help you be in the right places at the right times.

Lyft's PowerDriver Bonus

Lyft was the first to offer a driver bonus program encouraging drivers to use its platform more than those of its competitors. The PowerDriver Bonus program allows you to keep a higher percentage of your fare (Lyft takes a smaller cut) provided you accept a certain number of riders each week. Each city has different standards for the PowerDriver Bonus program. In my city, Lyft offers the PowerDriver Bonus 10 program, which requires that you take fifty trips, fifteen of which must be during defined peak hours, with a 90 percent acceptance rating or higher on all fifty rides. Should you meet this threshold, Lyft will only take a 10 percent cut of your fares for the week, as opposed to the usual 20 percent. My city also has the PowerDriver Bonus 20 program, which requires you to accept sixty-five riders in a week, twenty of which must be during defined peak periods, with a 90 percent acceptance rate on all sixty-five rides. Should you meet the requirements, Lyft won't take any cut of your fares, allowing you to keep everything you earned!

Uber's Bonus

Uber has followed suit in many cities, offering similar bonus programs where you'll earn extra money for accepting X number of rides during defined peak times during the week. In my city, Uber currently offers an extra $120 for driving forty rides during peak times in one week

Summary

The second step in boosting and maximizing your profits is to catch as many Surge and Primetime rides as possible. Study any data Uber or Lyft sends you and take advantage of third party apps at the iTunes and Google Play stores to help you be in the right places at the right times. Take advantage of Lyft's PowerDriver Bonus program and of Uber offers in your city to retain more of your earnings.

Driving Forward

Boost your profits by learning how to Ride the Surge and take advantage of Lyft and Uber's driver bonus programs.

- Continue to study the rider apps and Surge and Prime-time third party apps to learn the hot places and hot times. Check them each hour over the course of a week to build up longitudinal data.

- Read through any charts of peak earning driving hours that Uber and Lyft send.

- Take note of Lyft's PowerDriver Bonus program for your city and any comparable bonus program from Uber and the "peak driving times" required to earn the bonuses.

- Plan on your calendar to drive during these hours, your schedule permitting.

CHAPTER 23

RIGHT PLACE, RIGHT TIME

"Luck is being in the right place at the right time, but location and timing are to some extent under our control."

— Natasha Josefowitz

The Rearview Mirror

In the last chapter, I talked about Riding the Surge and Primetime as well as taking advantage of Driver Bonus programs that reward you for giving a set number of rides during defined peak demand periods. In this chapter, I will quickly review concepts learned in Chapter 12 about being in the right place at the right time and review some of the right places to be and the right times to be there.

DRIVING PROFITS AND MAKING BANK

Airports

You'll want to be at the airport during flight arrival times. Airlines stick to the same relative flight schedule each day and week, but third party apps let you track flight arrival times at your airport to help you be in the place where weary travelers will need a ride to their accommodations.

Tourist Areas and Attractions

Tourist areas and hotel districts are always full of tourists in need of a ride to attractions or restaurants. Tourist attractions are also a great place to be at closing time because tourists will need rides back to their hotels. The farther the attraction is from the hotel, the better.

Bar Districts

Bars and nightclubs are full of people too impaired to drive who are in need of a safe ride home. Closing times at these places typically cause a Surge. Get to know all the popular bars and nightclubs so you can be in place at closing time to make the most money.

Concert and Event Venues

Concert and sports venues are also often full of people in need of a ride home, especially if they enjoyed too much beer. Get to know the schedule of shows, matches, and events at the major venues in your town, and plan to be in place at the end of them in order to catch lots of potential riders.

University Dorms and Housing Areas

University and college campuses are always full of carless students in need of rides home, to part-time jobs, or, if living on campus, to off-campus entertainment. Be in place when classes let out, sporting events end, or at residence halls on weekends.

End of Shift

Commuters are in need of rides to and from work daily! Be in place in business districts, retail centers, military bases, hotel districts, or hospitals at shift changes to take these weary workers home.

Bad Weather

Bad weather equals lots of people not wanting to take public transportation like they normally would. If it starts to rain, snow, or storm, and you're not scared of driving in bad weather, get on the road because Surges will be going up.

Summary

Being in the right place at the right time increases your likelihood of being on hand when a Surge or Primetime occurs. Flight arrival times at airports; closing times at tourist attractions, bars, nightclubs, concerts, and sporting events; and shift change times in business, hotel, retail districts, hospitals, and military installations are just some of the examples of the right places to be at the right times.

Driving Forward

Knowing your town and what's happening in it helps you to know the right places and times to catch Surges and Primetimes. Let's continue to study your town as we did in Chapter 12.

- Research the major concert and sports venues in your area and note days and times of scheduled events.

- Research the major bars and nightclubs and their closing times.

- Research and know the military installations, convenient gate locations, and pickup areas.

- Research the airport area, designated waiting areas, and flight arrival schedules.

CHAPTER 24
REFERRAL PROGRAMS

"Nothing influences people more than a recommendation from a trusted friend. A trusted referral influences people more than the best broadcast message. A trusted referral is the Holy Grail of advertising."

— Mark Zuckerberg

The Rearview Mirror

In the last chapter, I reviewed popular high demand places and high demand times in most towns to help you set yourself up to be in the right places at the right times to get the best possible rides. In this chapter, I will discuss the next biggest revenue stream available to rideshare drivers—new driver and new passenger referrals.

Refer New Drivers

Both Uber and Lyft offer very generous referral bonuses to drivers who are able to recruit new drivers. Typically, to qualify for the bonus, your referral will need to enter your promotional code/referral number when applying on the Uber or Lyft website or click on your referral link on the web. Once the referral passes all the requirements and becomes an official driver, he or she will need to complete a set number of rides within a given timeframe, typically between thirty and forty rides within thirty days. The standard bonus range is from $50 to $200 in most cities.

Both the Uber and Lyft apps, and your driver dashboard on both sites, allows you to share your referral links and codes to your social, email, and text contacts.

During times when Uber or Lyft are in need of more drivers, they may offer huge promotional bonuses far beyond the standard, i.e., $500 per new sign-up or some type of scaled promotion such as $1,000 for three new sign-ups, $1,500 for four new

REFERRAL PROGRAMS

sign-ups, etc. Keep an eye on your email or text notifications for current recruitment bonus promotions available in your city.

I've been able to supplement my income quite generously over the past year by recruiting friends as fellow drivers.

Refer New Riders

In addition to signing up new drivers, you can also supplement your income nicely with passenger referrals. Encouraging family and friends to use Uber or Lyft helps to build business opportunities for all rideshare drivers by growing the user base in your community.

For passenger referrals, Uber and Lyft will pay cash bonuses as part of your weekly payout or credit you with ride credits for your personal use, depending on your city. In either event, you can supplement your driving income nicely with this referral revenue stream.

Lucrative Business

Some drivers supplement their incomes incredibly through referrals or forgo driving altogether to build their businesses through referrals alone.

39

"The Uber King," Joseph Ziyaee, famously made more than $90,000 in six months strictly off of new driver referrals. Numerous articles were published sharing his story.

Social Media

You can employ several strategies for advertising your referral business. The simplest is sharing your referral code on social media—Facebook, Twitter, Instagram, Pinterest, etc. Make an image with your referral codes to post on image sites like IG or Pinterest. If you don't have a graphics program like Photoshop, you can use a web app like Canva to make images for free. Each and every weekend, post your rider referral codes. Before any major concerts or sporting events in your town, post your rider referral codes. During any major driver recruitment push, post your driver referral codes. Social media is your friend when it comes to getting the word out about anything.

Business Cards

You'll also want to print out business cards with your referral codes on them to hand out. A business card is a basic tool for any business person—as an independent rideshare contractor, you are a business owner. Hand these cards out to people—

passengers who take rides with you, at church, at the gym, and at parties. Wherever you go, hand out your business card.

Vistaprint offers a convenient, online platform to order and print out new business cards, allowing you to save your card designs in your account for quick reorders.

Summary

In this chapter, I discussed how you can boost your business earnings through referring both new drivers and new passengers to Uber and Lyft, plus some strategies you can use to earn referrals. Leveraging social media and printing and handing out business cards with your referral code are two easy business-building strategies you can use to earn referral code income.

Driving Forward

Let's boost your profits by referring new drivers and new riders to Uber and Lyft. Complete the following exercises.

1. Learn about the Uber and Lyft driver and passenger referral programs in your city.

2. Reach out to twenty friends whom you think would be interested in driving part-time or full-time (recently un-

employed).

3. Share your referral codes on your social media regularly (at least once a week).

4. Print business cards with your referral codes on them.

CHAPTER 25
SELL ITEMS IN YOUR CAR

"It's not about having the right opportunities.
It's about handling the opportunities right."

— Mark Hunter

The Rearview Mirror

In the last chapter, I talked about how you can use Uber and Lyft's built-in new driver and new passenger referral systems to boost your earnings. In this chapter, I will discuss boosting your earnings by selling products to your riders.

The Proper Way to Sell

Many drivers supplement their incomes through in-car sales

of products. Some do so quite substantially, like Gavin Escolar, whom I'll mention more about below.

You can employ some of these techniques as well, but be careful. Before I get into discussing sales to passengers, let's quickly distinguish between the *right* way and the *wrong* way to sell.

One of the attractive things about using rideshare as a sales platform is the fact that you have a captive audience to pitch your products or services to for about ten minutes or so. This is good on the driver's end. On the passenger's end, the last thing she is looking for is a sales pitch she can't get away from. Do not turn your ride into a ten-minute infomercial. It will earn you lots of dings on the Professionalism rating.

Use your ride as a way to *suggest,* to bring up gently, what it is you do or have to sell, but under no conditions should you be hard selling riders and making your business offerings the focus of the ride. The focus of the ride should always be on meeting the rider's needs. If anything you happen to offer meets his or her needs, you're golden. If not, don't push it. Less is definitely more in this case.

Things That Sell

When it comes to things that sell to riders, it can come down to the basics. Food and clothing always sell.

Snack Foods

Food and drink sells—always. Prepackaged foods like chips, trail mixes, or other snacks make popular sale items, especially for hungry travelers or folks who spent a night out clubbing. In its early days, Uber made its reputation for luxury service and amenities through drivers offering bottled water or candies for free. Many entrepreneurial drivers took things further and offered snacks for sale, many offering homemade baked goods, fresh sandwiches, or other finger foods. Beware, though, that if you are selling perishable foods, you may be subject to health regulations and other cottage food laws.

T-Shirts

T-shirts are always a big seller. People always need or want clothes—particularly tourists who may be looking for keepsakes of their travels. If you can produce or procure T-shirts highlighting your city, you may be able to snag a few sales here and there, given the number of tourists you'll be picking up daily.

Jewelry

Fashion accessories are always big sellers. Quite famously, California jewelry designer and Uber driver Gavin Escolar made

$252,000 selling jewelry during Uber rides—turning his car into a mobile showroom. Numerous news stories were published highlighting his story (Google it)! Many of you may be Etsy store-owners or have a family member who runs an Etsy jewelry business. If you're a part of an Etsy family, there is good potential for making sales locally from the comfort of your car.

Tourist Guides and Keepsakes

Any other tourist keepsakes or guides will sell well. Tourists are in need of good information on places to visit and keepsakes to take home. If you're able to stock and display any of these in your car, you'll make sales.

Artists

If you're a working artist moonlighting as a rideshare driver, you'll also have a great opportunity to showcase your work to riders and try to make sales. If you're a graphic artist, painter, photographer, etc., you can display and sell your digital art, postcards, etc. If you're a musician with an album out, stock CDs and play your music while driving. If you're an author with published books, keep copies available and on display. Keep any brochures or flyers promoting upcoming shows or exhibitions to hand out. Tourists and commuters alike are always looking for things to do.

Card Readers

If you are looking at conducting in car sales, you'll definitely want to invest in a card payment system. Square, PayPal Here, and Intuit GoPayment are three popular platforms available that turn your smartphone into a credit card processing terminal with a plug-in reader and phone app.

Summary

In this chapter, we looked at boosting your profits through product sales. To succeed, you'll need to balance your sales with keeping yourself from becoming a driving infomercial and risking earning "Unprofessional" ratings and reviews from riders. Things such as snack foods, T-shirts, jewelry, and any other tourist keepsakes will sell well. Artists can use the opportunity to showcase their artwork, music, or comedy. If you are looking to do in-car sales, you will want to invest in getting a credit card reader to facilitate payments.

Driving Forward

Let's boost your profits by brainstorming products you can sell to passengers.

1. Knowing the types of people who take rideshare rides,

what types of products can you develop for in car sales?

2. What are ways you can soft sell these products so riders will be interested rather than turned off by your sales promotions?

CHAPTER 26

BUILD A RETURN CLIENTELE AND LEVERAGE OTHER BUSINESS OPPORTUNITIES

"Don't wait for extraordinary opportunities. Seize common occasions and make them great. Weak men wait for opportunities; strong men make them."

— Orison Swett Marden

The Rearview Mirror

In the last chapter, I talked about using product sales to boost your earnings and driving profits. In this chapter, I'll discuss building a return clientele and the art of upselling on any additional services you may offer.

The Art of Conversation

Before I get into promoting your additional services or businesses, I want to return to and reemphasize the art of conversation and meeting your passengers' immediate needs. Again, do not, under any circumstances, turn your ride into an infomercial—that will earn you bad ratings very quickly and increase hits on the "Unprofessional" ratings standard from Uber and Lyft.

Master the art of conversation, and when dealing with your passengers, learn what it is they want and need in the here and now. If any of their needs come up in conversation and can be met by something you offer as a driver or in your other professional life, then the door is open to make an offer—but not beforehand.

People will always do business with folks they trust and like. Use your conversation to impress upon your riders that you care about their needs and can meet them. If you can do this, they will remember you and be willing to contact you again for future needs.

Business Cards

As an independent rideshare contractor or other type of business professional, you should have business cards handy to promote any of your ridesharing and transportation ventures. In your other professional life (real estate, insurance sales, general contracting, catering, jewelry making, direct selling, or multi-level marketing), you should also have business cards.

On your rideshare and transportation business cards, you need to list at a minimum:

- Your name

- Your contact information

- Range of services you offer (I'll discuss possibilities later in this chapter)

- Referral codes for Uber, Lyft, or anything else relevant

Always keep stacks of business cards on hand in your car(s) to give out to passengers.

At the end of your ride and conversation with passengers, if you feel there's any potential to work with them again, give them your card(s). In the rest of this chapter, I will discuss potential spin-off business you can start to think about and offer to riders.

DRIVING PROFITS AND MAKING BANK

Tourists

As mentioned earlier, you'll be dealing with tourists quite a bit. One of the first things you'll want to find out from tourists is how long they'll be in town. You know that tourists will always need a ride, whether it's something as simple as getting back to the airport or going to the next tourist attraction on their itinerary. If you can develop a good enough relationship with them on your first ride, you may be able to cultivate return business.

Remote Tourist Drop Offs

If dropping tourists off in a more remote part of town where there are minimal rideshare opportunities, leave them your business card with an offer to come pick them up when they are done. Because there's no one else out there, and if you're close enough to them, or willing to drive back for them, the math may work out in your favor, especially if you know the return fare will be relatively high.

Private Tours

Many rideshare drivers supplement their income by selling *private tours* to tourists. Tourists, more than anything else, are searching for an *authentic* local experience, so if you know your town well enough, you're more than qualified to be a private tour guide. You'll be able to meet two of their needs: (1) show them the sights, tastes, and sounds of your town, and (2) get them around. With this venture, you'll be able to charge a nice premium for your driving, time, and local expertise.

Here are some popular types of tours you can explore offering if you are interested and have the expertise to do so:

- **Historical and Cultural Tours:** Do you know the history of your town and its people? Take tourists to all the famous historical landmarks important to your town's history and its people.

- **Food Tours:** People love to and need to eat! Do you know all the great foodie spots in town? Make a day of driving tourists to all the spots that serve the best food. Breakfast, lunch, dinner, snacks, and/or desserts!

- **Scenic/Eco Tours:** Do you know all the scenic spots in your town? Majestic forests? Waterfalls? Scenic lookouts? Safe animal encounters? People love to see things they cannot see at home. Think of all the great scenic and eco-spots in your town that tourists may be interested in seeing.

- **Movie/Film Tours:** We all love our Hollywood! If you happen to live in a town where a famous movie or TV series was filmed, you may generate some nice business taking people to filming locations they may remember seeing. Help folks vicariously chase the stars, or recall those epic moments they saw on the small or big screen!

If, in your conversation, you find the tourists will be in town for a few days, you have a great opportunity to offer them a chance to use you for a private tour. This is especially the case if they start to ask you for recommendations on places to visit or eat. They will obviously need a way to get there. If you can demonstrate a solid understanding of places around town and a comfortable personality, you stand a good chance of earning a booking.

Take some time to ponder your knowledge and inclination toward some local sites and put together a brochure listing offerings of tours you're willing to give and rates you'd charge for your time. Research other tour companies to see their rates and offerings to be sure you're priced competitively.

Once you've developed a brochure, keep copies of it in your car and hand them out as appropriate, along with your business cards.

One note on private tours. If you do choose to get into the private tour business, you will want to consider strongly looking into commercial driver's insurance to limit your liability in the event of an accident. You are not on Uber or Lyft time (unless you keep things on app while driving, at which point you are okay). If you are doing tours off app as a legitimate side business, definitely look at covering yourself through a commercial policy. Your personal auto policy would not apply or cover you for any damages in this situation because you are engaged in commercial activity.

Local Regulars

As mentioned earlier, you'll be driving many of the same riders, particularly if you drive the same schedule each day. You'll be taking people to and from work, school, and home. You'll also be taking people to run errands or to doctors' appointments. Some folks enjoy working with someone they know and trust to get them to the places they need to be. Many folks may inquire with you privately as to whether you'd be willing to take them or their loved ones for their regular appointments, especially if they are carless. They may need a reliable ride to get their kids to and from school daily if there's no one in the family who can take them. They may need a reliable ride to get their elderly parent or grandparent to weekly doctor's visits or to go grocery shopping. They may want a reliable, regular person to pick up their child or spouse from a late work shift instead of relying on public transportation.

Guaranteed, recurring business from people you have a relationship with is a good thing! As the proverb goes, "A bird in the hand is always worth two in the bush." Many folks choose to schedule and book these types of rides off app and deal directly with the rider on a cash basis, thus cutting out Uber or Lyft. Or you can keep things on app. If you do, you'll need to work the request system and ensure the ride is requested in your presence, while you are online, to match directly (this may take a few tries). Gaming the matching system is discouraged by Uber and Lyft, and it is considered a violation of service, so know and be aware of that if you choose to go that route.

Consider charging a premium for these rides because you will need to account for your off-app time and make sure you can make your pre-arranged rides—you won't be able to accept any requests for at least forty-five minutes prior to a pre-arranged ride. If you're taking folks to run errands or to doctor appointments, and they want you to wait for them, you'll also need to account for waiting time as well. It's best to charge an hourly rate for your time doing the job from when you leave home to pick them up through the time you drop them off. Many of these folks, because you are providing a value-added service, will also tip you very generously—because they depend on you. I earned some extremely generous fares and tips taking elderly folks for weekly grocery runs and doctors' appointments. If you can develop a recurring clientele, you can make a decent side income while completely bypassing Uber and/or Lyft.

Once again, a note on insurance. Much like with private tours, unless you are keeping things on app, you are engaged in commercial activity and your personal auto insurance policy may not cover you in the event of an accident. If you find yourself growing a steady clientele of off-app bookings, you may consider looking into commercial driver's insurance to limit your liability.

Your Other Business Ventures

As alluded to in the last chapter, rideshare is a great venue to "feel out" and qualify folks for your other services since you have approximately ten minutes of quality time with them to get to know them and ascertain their needs. You don't want to turn your ride into a driving infomercial, but you do have an opportunity to get to know people and see whether they may be in the market for anything you happen to be offering. Here is where mastering the art of conversation comes in. More often than not during your ride, your passengers will ask, "Do you do anything else besides driving?" or you'll have a chance to volunteer this information as a follow up if you ask them, "What do you do?" At that point, everything becomes fair game, so you can introduce any of your other ventures.

Rideshare is a great lead generator. It sure beats cold calling! Here are some of the service industries you may be in, or self-employed in, that may intersect with your rideshare gig and help build your clientele.

- **Real Estate:** A lot of riders may be looking to buy or sell a home in the near future. If you are a property manager, your passenger or a loved one may be looking for a place to rent.

- **Insurance:** Home, renters', auto, life, or long-term care— we all need a policy and will be glad to go with a company that offers the best rates.

- **Car Sales:** Most of these people, especially if they're locals, are carless and may be looking at some point.

- **Home, Auto, and Appliance Repair:** We all have something that needs repairs around the house.

- **Personal Training, Yoga, Pilates, CrossFit, etc.:** Everyone wants to get in better shape and may be looking for a good teacher and class—perhaps yours?

- **Food Service and Catering:** Everybody needs to eat!

Whether you own a restaurant, food truck, or catering business, everyone loves a good meal! Bonus points if you keep samples in your car.

- **Hair, Nails, Massage:** Everyone wants to look and feel better, and if your rider is not attached to anyone in particular and you give a good vibe, he or she may be willing to try out a session with you.

- **MLM, Direct Sales:** People need extra money or a good product that can make them feel better or solve some problem in their lives. Whether you're selling dietary supplements, weight loss shakes, exercise programs, essential oils, or beauty products, you and the company you represent may be the answer to your passengers' prayers.

Summary

In this chapter, I talked about how you can build up return clientele and ways you can leverage the needs of tourists or locals to develop lucrative, recurring business. Whether you're selling private tours to tourists or much needed transportation for carless residents to do their grocery shopping, attend doctor's appointments, or get home safely from work late in the evenings, ample opportunity exists to grow and develop recurring business if you can develop trust with riders. If you're driving part-time and have your own full-time endeavors outside of ridesharing, you can also use this opportunity to promote and share your full-time ventures, whether you work in real estate, finance, repair work, sales, health, beauty, or fitness.

Driving Forward

Let's boost your profits by helping you develop your conversation skills and potential tour packages.

- Brainstorm potential private tours and rates you can offer tourists. Develop a sample menu and brochure of your offerings.

- Order business cards if you've not already done so.

- Practice your conversation skills with people. Find a classmate, friend, or family member to role-play with. Start with simple questions such as, "What do you do for a living? Are you in school? Where do you work?"

- Practice conversing with a tourist. Find a classmate, friend, or family member to role-play with. "How long are you in town for?" Develop a quick pitch for places to visit, places to eat.

- From there, see whether you can boil down what you do into a few sentences. "Besides driving, I also _____. Would you be interested, or do you know anyone who needs ____?"

- If you see yourself doing tours, develop a package of offerings and rates.

PART V
THE NOT-SO-GLAMOROUS LIFE

CHAPTER 27
PITFALLS OF RIDESHARING

"When life is real, it's not going to be smooth."

— Mary J. Blige

The Rearview Mirror

In the previous section, I discussed strategies to boost your earnings, including finding Surges/Primetimes, earning driver bonuses, selling products, or upselling passengers to your own premium services and other offerings. In this section, I will discuss the not-so-glamorous side of ridesharing, share some of the pitfalls to watch out for, and look at how to deal with some of the difficult situations you'll encounter.

DRIVING PROFITS AND MAKING BANK

Obnoxious People

If you choose to drive in the evenings and/or at night, especially on weekends, you'll spend a good deal of time dealing with drunk people. Having encountered drunks, we all know they can range from amusing to obnoxious to downright dangerous. The fact of the matter is, though, if you're going to be on the road during peak drinking and party hours, you will need to deal with drunks.

In Chapter 28, I will go over some safety techniques and help you develop a safety plan for yourself.

Wear and Tear on Your Car

Another major downside is the inevitable wear and tear on your car. Your upholstery will wear down quickly. Should passengers have accidents with food or bodily fluids in your car, you'll need to clean it up. (You can recover a cleaning fee from the passenger by reporting the incident to Uber or Lyft.)

The additional miles on the road will wear down your car quicker. You'll need to rotate your tires and change them more often. You'll need to service your car more often, be it changing the oil, other fluids, or parts. Can you make enough with your town's rideshare rates to pay for these costs? It's not just the gas you need to think about. We all know how costly car repairs and service can be. As a driver, you'll need to put a lot more money and time into your vehicle!

Dangers of the Road

Traffic

Part of being a rideshare driver is increased time on the road, and a side effect of that is dealing with increased risks and hassles.

It should go without saying, if you're not a fan of traffic, rideshare driving may not be for you—at all. If you choose to be on the road during peak hours, you will get stuck in traffic. Roadwork. Construction. Accidents. You'll deal with them every day, far more than just the average commuter. Sure, you'll be *paid* to sit in traffic, which does make it better and more bearable, but if you're not a traffic type of person, you'll grow to hate it pretty fast —unless you drive in non-peak traffic hours.

Law Enforcement Traffic Stops

One of the side effects of continuously being on the road is a higher chance of being subject to a law enforcement traffic stop. You're on the road more often, thus there's a greater chance you may accidentally (or intentionally) violate a traffic law. In the twenty years I drove prior to being a rideshare driver, I was only ever stopped for violating a traffic law once. However, in my first year as a rideshare driver, I had three traffic stops. Be aware of all applicable traffic laws and road signs. In Chapter 30, I will cover in depth how to deal with and interact with law enforcement on the road and some of the traffic law pitfalls you need to watch out for.

Potential for Car Accidents

And last but not least, being on the road more, unfortunately, does put you at a much higher risk for being involved in a traffic accident. Whether it's your fault, the other driver's fault, a pedestrian's fault, or a freak accident beyond anyone's control, you still stand higher chance of being in a car accident. In my twenty years of driving prior to rideshare driving, I'd only ever been in three accidents—ever. In one year of rideshare driving, I was in three accidents! Thankfully, nothing major happened, but still, an accident is an accident and it is a headache to deal with!

PITFALLS OF RIDESHARING

Inaccurate or Unsafe Pickup Points

As mentioned in Chapter 13, you will also deal regularly with wrong pickup locations due to technical or human error. On occasion, you'll also be asked to pick up passengers at very unsafe locations or locations where pickups are prohibited, such as streets with no stopping or pullover signs, or secure or prohibited locations where pickups are not allowed like airports, boat harbors, or other secured sites. You will need to educate passengers or request they meet you in safer locations. Most of the time, folks are reasonable, but sometimes, they'll be very unreasonable and upset at not getting the door-to-door service they feel entitled to. And sometimes you'll spend quite some time hunting for them if they start to move from their pickup location or simply cannot articulate to you where they are.

Lyft's Pickup Radius

A unique aspect of being a Lyft driver is having to deal with Lyft's wide pickup radius. As mentioned earlier, you can get ride requests in excess of thirty minutes away from your location. As a driver, you are *not* compensated for your en route time, and you are always at risk of a passenger cancelling on you while you are in transit. Consequently, you stand the risk of driving

for a half hour or more only to be canceled on or to take someone for a five-minute ride.

Subject to Arbitrary Rate Changes

One of the major downsides to rideshare driving is being at the
mercy of the driving structures of Uber and Lyft. Both companies
(more so Uber, which forces Lyft to follow suit to remain compet-
itive) have been known to drop their rates to entice riders. Lower
rates, of course, mean lower payouts for you for doing the same
work. The theory goes that lower rates create more demand,
which means more fares per hour. That theory does not necessarily hold up since other factors affect demand. What does hold
up is that you make less per ride than you used to.

During my time as a driver, I went through one rate drop, and I
know it took a few months before demand evened out so I was
making *around* the same each hour that I had previously. Over
time, other things have also effected rates. Now, with full hind-
sight, I can say that I made way more as a driver back then than
I do now.

Being a part of the Uber and Lyft systems puts you at the mercy
of any arbitrary decisions they make. Lower rates will equal lower
payouts.

PITFALLS OF RIDESHARING

Breaking Even

At the end of the day, being a rideshare driver is a business. Statistics never lie. Most businesses fail. Depending on your market and your personal situation, there is a chance that this venture may not pay off for you.

In some markets, the base rates, mileage, and time multipliers are *very* low and each ride pays very little. Factoring in your gas, maintenance costs, and taxes, chances are you might make less than minimum wage or not even break even.

In some markets, the rider demand is simply not there. If you live in a huge metropolitan area, chances are you will have great demand. If you live in a sparsely populated area, there may not be enough demand to make a living. If you're looking to make side money, you should be okay. If your goal is to drive for your livelihood, you may still need to seek out part-time employment or other side ventures.

Some markets may be oversaturated with drivers. Business is always about supply and demand. Some markets may have a constant demand for rides, but there may be way too many drivers. Think about restaurants, food trucks, food stands, convenience stores, or clothing stores. People always need food, gas, and other necessities. But there's no shortage of places to get them.

DRIVING PROFITS AND MAKING BANK

Most restaurants fail. Sometimes restaurants, gas stations, or clothing stores are not profitable simply because the market is oversaturated. Rideshare supply and demand is cyclical. I've seen times when rides are very plentiful, and I've seen times when you could go a half hour or more without getting a ping because there's simply too many drivers on the road.

Factoring the costs of your car: car payments, insurance, gas, maintenance, and taxes—there may be times when you don't break even or you wind up in the hole.

Definitely treat rideshare driving as a business and keep proper track of your income and expenses. Apps like QuickBooks Self-Employed, Hudlr, etc. are great for this. (I will cover these and more in the appendices.)

Summary

In this chapter, I explained the not-so-glamorous things you'll deal with as a rideshare driver, including obnoxious passengers, constant traffic, higher risk of accidents and/or traffic stops, wear and tear on your car, flaky passengers, bad pickup locations, and being at the mercy of rate and payout drops. You'll also risk losing money. We're all in the business of making money, but sometimes, we lose. Given your situation, or the demand in your town, the numbers may not work in your favor. Rideshare driving can be very exciting and fun, but like anything else, it can be a hassle as well.

Driving Forward

Knowledge is power! Let's spend some time researching the rideshare market and traffic laws in your city and review some safety techniques to keep you on the road and profitable.

1. Research and review defensive driving techniques.

2. Research and know traffic laws for your city.

3. Research the rates Uber and Lyft charge in your city. Talk to other drivers about actual average per hour earnings.

CHAPTER 28
STAYING SAFE WHILE DRIVING

"Safety is a cheap and effective insurance policy."

— Author Unknown

The Rearview Mirror

In the last chapter, I discussed the pitfalls to rideshare driving. In this chapter, I will discuss driver safety tips and how you can put together a safety plan.

Set a Schedule and Let Loved Ones Know It

One of the first things you can do is set a work schedule and communicate it with your loved ones. Let your loved ones know when you'll be driving and when they can expect you back— like with any job or schedule. If you're not back at your expected time, or if they've not heard from you, it's time for them to start looking for you or contact the authorities.

Check in with Loved Ones

Like with most daily schedules, it's good to check in regularly throughout the day with a loved one, be it your significant other, parent, BFF, or roommate, just so someone knows you're okay. As long as the people who need to know you're okay, know you're okay, things are okay. If something is not okay, the best way to let them know, if you're unable to make contact, is for them not to hear from you when they expect to. At that point, they can initiate whatever process is necessary to find you and get you the help you need in the event something bad has happened.

Install a Dash Cam

Dash cams are increasingly becoming a popular tool for all drivers, not just rideshare drivers. As a safety practice, it is a best practice to install one in your vehicle, especially since they are becoming increasingly inexpensive.

The video evidence will be invaluable if you ever have any type of incident with a passenger, another driver, or a law enforcement officer. Video serves to protect you and your passengers.

Be aware that your local laws may require you to disclose to passengers and others they are being recorded. If that's the case, a simple sign in your car will probably suffice.

Again, dash cams are becoming increasingly affordable. The Falcon Zero F360, at $120 to $150 as of this printing, is the highly rated and reviewed model I personally use.

Refuse Sketchy Pickups

Always remember that ultimately *you are in charge*. You can refuse pickups. If you arrive to a pickup location and find that there are more passengers than your car can hold, and they try to convince you to let everyone in ("They'll sit on my lap. He'll ride in the trunk."), you can refuse. If the rider is way too drunk or combative and belligerent, you can refuse. If he is too dirty and you don't want your car to be a mess, you can refuse. You're the boss. You always have the right to refuse.

Kick Out Sketchy Passengers

Conversely, you also have the right to kick out passengers. If they're rude, combative, if you feel they're dangerous and your safety is at stake, or if, heaven forbid, they assault you (we've seen the YouTube videos), you certainly have the right to kick them out!

Report Problem Passengers

If you have a problem with a passenger, you should always report the incident and the passenger to Uber or Lyft. Both the app and the partner dashboards on the website have features to report bad passengers and bad trips. Doing so can get dangerous or inappropriate passengers banned from the Uber or Lyft platforms and negate any negative ratings they may have left about you.

Lyft maintains an emergency hotline number that's staffed 24/7. Save it to your phone: 855-865-9553.

Contact Law Enforcement

If it becomes necessary, contact law enforcement for assistance. If you live in a metropolitan area, there will be cops everywhere (you'll see them). Also, know where the nearest police precincts and stations are in each neighborhood. If an incident happens, law enforcement will be able to assist you whether you're attacked and need to file a police report, or a passenger refuses to exit your car and you need some help getting him or her to leave.

Summary

In this chapter, I shared safety tips and safety procedures as outlined by Uber and Lyft. Always be sure to communicate your whereabouts with loved ones. Install a dash cam for your safety. Remember that you are always in control of a ride and can refuse or end service at any time, refusing to pick up or kicking out sketchy passengers. Always remember to report dangerous or troublesome passengers to Uber or Lyft, either through the app or the website. Contact Lyft's emergency hotline if need be. Be sure the number is saved to your phone. As a final resort, contact law enforcement in the event of an emergency.

Driving Forward

Let's put together a safety plan for you so you can drive with confidence.

1. Order and install a dash cam for your car.
2. Note and know common areas police cars patrol and congregate.
3. Look up and know the locations of police precincts in your city.
4. Familiarize yourself with Uber and Lyft's apps and websites so you know how and where to report dangerous or troublesome passengers.
5. Save Lyft's emergency hotline number to your phone.

CHAPTER 29

DEALING WITH CAR ACCIDENTS

"My recent car accident was far less traumatic than dealing with my insurance company over the car accident claim."

— Pinterest Posting

The Rearview Mirror

In the last chapter, I discussed and developed a safety plan to help you drive with confidence and keep yourself safe on the road. While we try our best to remain safe, inevitably, accidents happen. In this chapter, I will discuss what to do when an accident occurs.

Contact Emergency Responders

First and foremost, if anyone is injured in your car or the other car, contact emergency personnel right away. Safety is the most important priority for everyone!

Have a Copy of Your Insurance Certificate

As you may recall from Chapter 9, both Uber and Lyft's insurance covers all rides taken while driving on their platforms. You are covered from the time you accept a ride request until the time you drop the passenger off. Uber uses the James River Insurance Company. Lyft uses Steadfast Insurance Company.

Uber and Lyft both provide copies of the insurance certificates on the app and through your driver partner dashboard. You should take the time to print copies and keep them in your glove compartment alongside your personal auto insurance.

Contact Law Enforcement

Secondly, you should contact law enforcement and file a traffic incident report. Some states may require you to do this by law, but even if they don't, it is a best practice to protect yourself. Documentation by law enforcement will help with any legal or insurance claims. Law enforcement presence can also help diffuse any situations with the other party. Dealing with your insurance company will be easier with law enforcement documentation of the accident.

Contact Uber or Lyft

Third, be sure to contact Uber or Lyft. By company policy and protocol, both Uber and Lyft require driver partners to contact them in case of emergency. You can contact them through your mobile app or the driver dashboard on the web. In the case of Lyft, you can call its twenty-four-hour emergency hotline to report an accident or any type of safety incident.

Lyft's hotline number is: 855-865-9553.

Both companies, as part of their insurance process, will require you to verify that you have personal auto coverage on your vehicle, and they will have you submit pictures of your vehicle's damages as part of the claim initiation process.

File Claim with Rideshare Insurance Companies

Once you've reported your accident and initiated the claims process, both Uber and Lyft will put you in touch with their insurance companies. Again, Uber uses the James River Insurance Company. Lyft uses Steadfast Insurance Company.

Both companies will require pictures of damages to your car for estimating insurance benefit payouts.

Follow Up with Insurance Companies

As with many insurance companies, you will want to be sure to follow up with them on the progress of your claim if you do not hear from them or receive your payout. Claims representatives will typically leave you a direct phone number and email address, and they are usually very responsive to messages.

Deductibles

Uber and Lyft have high deductibles on their insurance. Uber has a $1,000 deductible, and Lyft has a $2,500 deductible. As a business owner, you should keep cash to cover deductibles in your business savings account to avoid precarious financial positions should you have an accident and be forced to pay a substantial deductible. You can always finance or make installment payments to repair shops, but it's not pleasant and you do wind up paying more.

Reinstate Your Car

Once your car is repaired, you will either need to resubmit pictures or pass a safety inspection to get your car reactivated on the Uber or Lyft platforms.

Summary

In this chapter, I gave you a rundown of how to deal with car accidents and the insurance claim process for Uber and Lyft should you get into a traffic accident. Be sure to contact emergency responders if anyone is hurt. Contact law enforcement to file a traffic collision report so you have documentation for any liability claims, to diffuse any situation with the other party, and to provide documentation for insurance claims. Contact Uber and Lyft through the app, driver dashboard, or in the case of Lyft, its twenty-four-hour emergency hotline. Be sure your personal auto insurance is up to date, and submit verification to Uber and/or Lyft that you're covered. Submit pictures to Uber and Lyft and their insurance companies for benefit estimation. Be sure to carry enough in savings to cover the deductible amounts—$1,000.00 for Uber, $2,500.00 for Lyft. Follow up with the insurance companies regarding payouts if you are not receiving them in a timely fashion. Resubmit photos or complete a safety check to reactivate your car.

Driving Forward

Let's get you ready to deal with a traffic incident more effectively.

1. Print copies of Uber and Lyft insurance certificates and put them in your car(s) alongside your personal insurance.

2. Save the Lyft emergency hotline number to your phone.

CHAPTER 30

DEALING WITH LAW ENFORCEMENT

"Anybody who thinks talk is cheap has never
argued with a traffic cop."

— Henny Youngman

The Rearview Mirror

In the last chapter, I discussed how to handle things in the event that you are in a traffic accident. In this chapter, I will discuss how to interact with law enforcement in the event that you are pulled over.

DRIVING PROFITS AND MAKING BANK

Know the Traffic Laws

One of the things about being on the road more is that the probability of interacting with law enforcement increases exponentially. In the first year I drove for Uber and Lyft, I was pulled over three times by cops for traffic violations. I'd been driving for twenty-two years beforehand and had only been pulled over three times in all those years. Being on the road constantly means your chances of being pulled over and needing to interact with a cop will go up.

You can decrease your chances of traffic stops by knowing the traffic laws of your city and state and complying with them. Here are some laws to be aware of and read up on for your city.

Hands-Free Device Laws

Most jurisdictions now have some type of mobile device law requiring drivers to use a hands-free set or mount while driving to ensure they are not distracted by holding a device that can slow their reaction time and cause them to take their eyes off the road. Uber and Lyft policies also dictate that you use a hands-free device or phone mount to protect your and passengers' safety. Thousands of drivers are pulled over each day for violating this law and safety practice. And in 2014, *USA Today* reported that one quarter of all traffic accidents were caused by cellphone use, so be sure you are in compliance with both Uber/Lyft's policy and the nearly ubiquitous laws.

Seatbelt Laws

Most jurisdictions now require all front seat passengers to wear seatbelts. Many jurisdictions also require backseat passengers to use a seatbelt as well. Per Uber and Lyft policy, you *must* have functioning seatbelts in the front and back seats. Be sure to wear your seatbelt at all times, and enforce the policy of requiring your passengers to wear their seatbelts as well. As the driver, you are liable for the conduct of your passengers, and you will be stopped and cited in the event that your passengers are not wearing seatbelts as the law dictates.

Child Seat Laws

Many jurisdictions also have child safety seat laws requiring children under certain ages or certain heights/weights to be strapped into a child safety seat. Occasionally, you may pick up passengers with children, whether they are tourists on vacation or residents taking their child to school, a doctor's appointment, or to run errands. If the child is still of safety seat age or height/weight, be sure the passenger provides a safety seat. Keep one in your trunk to accommodate passengers who may not be prepared. If they do not have a safety seat, and you do not have one, you risk a traffic stop should an officer observe a child riding without one. Remember, as the driver, you are responsible for ensuring you and your passengers are in compliance with the law.

Open Container Laws

In most jurisdictions, it is illegal to operate a motor vehicle with an open container of alcohol, regardless of whether it belongs to a passenger or, especially, you as the driver. This is especially a problem on weekends when you are mostly driving party-goers to and from nightclubs and bars. Many passengers will want to enter your car with their drinks. Be aware of and enforce any open container laws your jurisdiction may have. Again, you are liable for the conduct of your passengers, and you will need to face and pay any traffic fines (or worse) should you be stopped. Be aware that many police departments and sheriffs' deputies set up roadblocks on the weekend to catch or deter drunk drivers.

If your passenger has an open container in your car, you are in for trouble. Know the law. Abide by it. Enforce it.

Narcotics Laws

Finally, be aware of the narcotics laws in your jurisdiction. Sometimes, your passengers may come in and, unbeknownst to you, be carrying illegal substances—and in worst-case scenarios, leave them behind in your car. Do your best to monitor the activities of your passengers and to check and clean out your car regularly after dropping passengers off. If a passenger starts smoking or doing drugs during your ride, immediately pull over, end the ride, and boot him from your car. If you need assistance, contact law enforcement. Regularly inspect your car after a certain number of rides or during downtimes to ensure it is "clean" both in the traditional sense and in the explicit sense. If you are pulled over and an officer smells or observes an illegal substance, you will be arrested, held liable, and be required to go through the hassle of explaining your status as an innocent Uber or Lyft driver who picked up a bad ride.

Ensure Passengers Comply with Laws

Let it be reiterated one final time. Be sure that not only you are in compliance with all traffic laws, but that all your passengers are as well. If there are seatbelt laws, make sure passengers are buckled up. If they are bringing children and the law dictates their child be in a safety seat, make sure they have a safety seat or cancel the ride. If they are bringing open containers into your car, refuse entry or make sure they leave their drinks behind. If they are coming in with drugs, deny them entry or make sure they leave the drugs behind, and make sure you double-check after drop off to ensure your car is "clean." You, as the driver, are responsible for ensuring your car, yourself, and your passengers are in compliance with traffic laws. You'll be the one getting pulled over, paying the fine, and going to court if you and your passengers are not.

Follow Traffic Signs

As a driver, you are responsible for obeying all traffic laws and traffic signs at all hours of the day. This can pose a problem if you are driving in unfamiliar areas, especially during the evenings when traffic signs may be more difficult to read and see. In particular, though, be aware and on the lookout for these types of signs:

- **No Right Turn on Red:** Many streets do not allow right

turns on red, especially when turning might impede the traffic flow from the oncoming direction. Most of us are taught that it is okay to turn right on red at an intersection after either slowing or coming to a complete stop. This is true unless posted otherwise.

- **No Stopping:** Many major streets and thoroughfares do not allow cars to stop on the road to pick up or drop off passengers. This is a problem since many passengers may either request pickups from these locations or ask to be dropped off. If this is the case, pull off on a side street, if possible, to drop off or pick up your passenger.

- **Bus Only Lane:** Many streets have designated public transit only lanes. Signs will typically be posted that should alleviate problems. During night hours, though, these signs may be more difficult to see.

- **No U Turn:** Many intersections do not allow U turns. If you get a ride request from the opposite direction, you may want or need to make a U turn. If you're at a "No U Turn" intersection, you'll need to wait until you find a legal intersection to turn around.

DRIVING PROFITS AND MAKING BANK

Be Aware of Restricted Areas

It may take some time to learn where they are, but be aware of restricted pickup and drop-off areas in your town, such as airports, harbors, convention centers, parks, tourist attractions, and military bases. Some of these places may not allow ride-share drivers to drop off or pick up passengers or may have designated areas for drop offs and pickups. Depending on the officers on duty at the time, they may or may not be lenient or forgiving of driver ignorance.

Check with your local Uber office (if any) or online driver support groups in your area for information on restricted areas.

Interacting with Officers

In the event that you are stopped by a law enforcement officer, it is best to follow these three best practices:

1. **Comply with all instructions**. Beyond anything else, this is the most important thing. The media is full of stories, images, and videos of traffic stops gone wrong. You should always comply with instructions to avoid aggravating officers or facilitating an encounter gone wrong.

2. **Treat officers with respect**. Typically speaking, if you treat an officer with respect, he or she will do the same.

Officers by and large are honest and work with integrity. The officers portrayed in media stories are the exception and not the norm. I was stopped three times in my first year driving, and all of my encounters with the officers were positive, citations received aside. Always remember the officers are, like the rest of us, simply doing their jobs to the best of their abilities. If you are being pulled over, it is more than likely for a good and legitimate reason. Let the officer do his or her job.

3. **Keep your hands visible**. One of the hallmarks of "encounters gone wrong" are occupants not keeping their hands visible. An officer's worst fear is getting that one bad traffic stop where the car is filled with legit criminals who will pull guns and shoot a cop. You should always keep your hands visible. Once you are pulled over, get your license, registration, and insurance card ready, leave them in a visible area, and keep your hands visible to the officer.

Doing these three things will make your interaction with the officer more pleasant, and if you are lucky, will result in a *warning* and not a citation. Of my three traffic stops, I was only cited in two of them. The third officer let me off with a warning.

If Cited, Contact Uber or Lyft

If you are cited for something beyond your control, contact Uber or Lyft. Depending on the situation, the company may either pay your citation or help you get legal representation. Typically, if you are cited for passenger conduct (i.e., passenger not wearing a seatbelt) or for ending up in a restricted area because you didn't know any better, the company may reimburse you. Routine traffic stops such as speeding will not be reimbursed.

Legal Representation

As a best practice, you may want to consider having the name and number of an attorney on hand should you ever need representation. You can use family, friends, or classmates for referrals, or use a site like Martindale.com (the Yelp for attorneys) to find a good attorney. Another option is to sign up for a service like LegalShield, which provides you with 24/7 access to an attorney for any reason.

Summary

In this chapter, I provided best practice tips for interacting with law enforcement during traffic stops, including how to lower your chances of being stopped. You should be aware of and abide by all traffic laws in your jurisdiction and ensure your passengers are obeying the laws as well. Be aware of, read, and follow all posted traffic signs. Contact Uber or Lyft in the event of a traffic citation. Obey all instructions and cooperate with any officers who pull you over, keeping your hands visible at all times. Consider keeping an attorney's name and number handy or use a service like LegalShield in the event you need representation in traffic court.

Driving Forward

Let's get you ready to stay out of trouble with the law, but also prepared in the event that you are cited for a traffic violation.

1. Research and know your local traffic laws. Check your state's revised statutes and your city or county's traffic ordinances for current laws.

2. Research a good attorney who deals with traffic laws. Ask family or friends for a referral, visit Martindale.com, or look into getting LegalShield. If you're interested in learning more about LegalShield, I'll be glad to provide you with more information.

PART VI
DRIVE ON

CHAPTER 31

RIDESHARE START-UPS TO KEEP AN EYE ON

"Here comes a new challenger!"

— Street Fighter

The Rearview Mirror

In the previous section, I shared the not-so-glamorous aspects of life as a rideshare driver. In this section, I will identify some additional opportunities and possibilities you can take advantage of. In this specific chapter, I will share some of the rideshare companies you will want to keep an eye on.

Companies to Watch

As the rideshare economy matures, we see more and more companies emerging to take on Uber or Lyft or to find specific niches to call their own. Here are some companies to keep an eye on over the next few years.

Fare

Currently based in Phoenix, Arizona, and Austin, Texas, Fare allows riders to "favorite preferred" drivers, thereby allowing drivers to build up a clientele. The service also allows riders to preschedule rides.

Visit http://ridefare.com or download the app from the Apple App Store or Google Play Store on your iOS or Android device.

Fasten

Currently based in Boston, Massachusetts, and Austin, Texas, Fasten takes a flat, $1.00 commission on all rides, thus allowing drivers to keep more of each fare. No more giving away 20 or 25 percent. Fasten also does not penalize drivers for not taking rides.

Visit http://www.fasten.com or download the app from the Apple App Store or Google Play Store on your iOS or Android device.

RIDESHARE START-UPS TO KEEP AN EYE ON

GetMe

Currently available throughout Texas and in Las Vegas, Nevada, with plans to expand to Chicago, Los Angeles, Denver, Atlanta, Nashville, Portland, and cities throughout Australia and Canada, GetMe is both a rideshare and a delivery service app. GetMe allows passengers to both pre-book rides and have "favorite" drivers, helping drivers build up a clientele.

Visit http://www.getme.com or download the app from the Apple App Store or Google Play Store on your iOS or Android device.

InstaRyde

Available only in Ontario, Canada, and Austin, Texas, InstaRyde only takes a 12.5 percent commission on rides.

Visit http://www.instaryde.com or download the app from the Apple App Store or Google Play Store on your iOS or Android device.

SafeHer

Currently based in Boston, Massachusetts, with expansion plans to D.C., Chicago, Los Angeles, and New York, SafeHer offers rides to women riders provided by women drivers.

Visit http://www.safeher.com or download the app from the Apple App Store or Google Play Store on your iOS or Android device.

SheRides

Currently based in New York, SheRides offers rides to women riders provided by women drivers.

Visit http://www.sheridesnyc.com or download the app from the Apple App Store or Google Play Store on your iOS or Android device.

Wingz

Currently available throughout California, Texas, and in Phoenix, Portland, and Seattle, Wingz specializes in pre-booked, airport rides. Riders can book directly with drivers.

Visit http://wingz.me or download the app from the Apple App Store or Google Play Store on your iOS or Android device.

Summary

In this chapter, we looked at several rideshare start-ups looking to compete with Uber and Lyft. Many of these services offer innovations such as allowing riders to choose favorite drivers, which allows drivers to build up clientele. Some take a smaller percentage of the fare from each ride, allowing drivers to take home more money per ride. Some allow passengers to pre-book rides directly with drivers. Many are competing in specific niches, such as airport rides or women-only drivers for women-only passengers.

Driving Forward

Let's take some time to look at the potential future of the rideshare business by checking out some of the rising rideshare companies.

1. Check out the websites for each of the rideshare services mentioned in this chapter.

2. If you live in a town served by these companies, consider signing up as a driver.

CHAPTER 32

BUSINESSES COMPLEMENTARY TO RIDESHARING

"To hell with circumstances; I create opportunities."

— Bruce Lee

The Rearview Mirror

In the last chapter, I shared several rideshare companies to keep an eye on in the next few years. In this chapter, I will highlight numerous other flexible business and income-making opportunities in the on-demand and sharing economies; some of them you've undoubtedly heard of (like Airbnb) and many others you may not have heard of.

DRIVING PROFITS AND MAKING BANK

Complementary Opportunities

Like the emerging rideshare companies discussed in the last chapter, keep in mind that most of these companies are still relatively new and in the start-up phase of their business cycles. Like many tech startups, they may be growing and expanding today and be out of business tomorrow. The on-demand and sharing economies are littered with the remains of failed companies (i.e., Sidecar, Homejoy, Washio, etc.).

Nevertheless, if you need additional flexible income opportunities *now*, and if these companies operate in your town, now is a good time to check them out and milk these opportunities.

Courier Delivery

Perhaps driving drunks or tourists isn't really your thing, or you're not big on small talk. As a delivery driver, you can still make the same, flexible money with your car (or in some cases bike, motorcycle, or scooter) and smartphone that you've come to expect from Uber or Lyft.

Whether you're delivering groceries, restaurant takeout, booze, prescriptions, or various other items from retailers and small businesses to customers, you can make decent side money as a courier/delivery driver for any of the various on-demand companies operating throughout the country. We'll cover the major ones in the next few pages.

Amazon Flex

Amazon Flex is the delivery service for the ubiquitous Amazon.com. It focuses on the Amazon Prime and Amazon Prime Now services. As a Flex driver, you'll be delivering Amazon packages, and in many markets, food from restaurants and other Amazon partner stores. To be a driver, you need to be twenty-one years of age or older, have a valid driver's license, and pass a background check. Amazon Flex is available in twenty-nine cities across the country.

Visit http://flex.amazon.com for more information.

Caviar

Caviar is a more recent entry into the crowded restaurant delivery market. Drivers have the option to deliver by car, truck, bike, scooter, or motorcycle. To qualify, you need to be eighteen years of age or older and have two years of driving experience. Caviar is available in fifteen cities.

Visit http://www.trycaviar.com for more information.

DRIVING PROFITS AND MAKING BANK

Deliv

Similar to Postmates (see below), Deliv couriers deliver items from retail stores. Unlike Postmates, you must have a car made after 2000. You'll also need to be at least eighteen years of age, have a valid driver's license, be able to lift fifty pounds, and pass a background check. Deliv is available in fifteen cities across the country.

Visit http://www.deliv.co for more information.

DoorDash

DoorDash was one of the first and is one of the biggest movers in the takeout food delivery market. As a DoorDash driver, you can deliver meals with your car, bicycle, scooter, or motorcycle. To qualify, you must be eighteen years of age or older, have one year of driving experience, a clean driving record, a valid driver's license, and personal insurance. DoorDash operates in twenty-five cities across the country.

Visit http://www.doordash.com for more information.

Favor

Favor drivers deliver anything from takeout orders to groceries and other retail goods. As a Favor "Runner" you can make deliveries by car, truck, bicycle, moped, or motorcycle. You need to be at least eighteen years of age or older. Favor operates in cities in Arizona, Colorado, Massachusetts, North Carolina, Tennessee, and Texas.

Visit http://favordelivery.com for more information.

GrubHub

GrubHub is the other market leader in the restaurant on-demand delivery business and operates in sixteen states. As a GrubHub driver, you'll only be able to make deliveries by car. To qualify, you need a valid driver's license, reliable car, auto insurance, and a clean driving record.

Visit http://www.grubhub.com for more information.

Instacart

Instacart was the pioneer and is the most well-known, on-demand grocery delivery service in the nation. As an Instacart "Shopper," you'll be picking up and delivering groceries for customers by car. To qualify, you'll need to be twenty-one years of age or older, able to lift thirty pounds, and have a reliable car. Instacart is available in twenty states.

Visit http://www.instacart.com for more information.

Postmates

Postmates is the current market leader in the on-demand courier market, comparable to Uber's dominance in the rideshare market. As a Postmates courier, you'll be delivering anything from takeout, to liquor, to prescriptions, and other items from convenience stores. As a plus, besides deliveries by car, you'll also have the option to deliver by bike, scooter, motorcycle, or on foot. As the market leader, Postmates is available in twenty-three states.

Check out http://postmates.com for more information.

Saucey

Saucey is an alcohol delivery service app that partners with liquor stores in the local community, allowing users to order online and have liquor delivered right to their doors. As a Saucey driver, you'll be shuttling booze from various stores in the community to customers. Service is currently provided in Los Angeles, San Diego, San Francisco, and Chicago.

BUSINESSES COMPLEMENTARY TO RIDESHARING

For more information visit http://sauceyapp.com.

Shipt

Shipt is a recent entry in the on-demand grocery delivery market. To qualify as a driver, you'll need to be eighteen years of age or older, be able to lift twenty-five pounds, have a valid driver's license, have a reliable car, and pass a background check. Shipt is currently available in nine states throughout the Southeast, and in Arizona, Texas, and Ohio.

Visit http://www.shipt.com for more information.

UberEATS

The final option I'll cover in the on-demand restaurant delivery business is UberEATS. Leveraging its network of rideshare drivers, one of Uber's first expansions was into the restaurant delivery market. UberEATS is available in twenty-five cities throughout the U.S. and also cities in Canada, Australia, and in London, Paris, and Singapore. If you're already an Uber driver in those cities, adding UberEATS is a quick and easy process.

Visit http://ubereats.com for more information.

DRIVING PROFITS AND MAKING BANK

UberRUSH

As the pioneer of the on-demand economy, Uber has tested courier services in various markets and has recently launched UberRUSH in San Francisco, Chicago, and New York City. As an UberRUSH courier, you'll be shuttling various packages between businesses and consumers.

Visit http://rush.uber.com for more information.

Tour Guide

The local personal tour guide business has seen mixed success matching travelers with locals who offer personalized tours or "local experiences" to travelers for a fee. The web is rife with sites featuring this service. Of all of these sites, Vayable is the most prominent and oldest.

Rideshare drivers who are doing well make a good portion of their money upselling personal tours guaranteeing travelers a ride and an authentic local view and experience.

To bolster your tour or local experience business, consider posting listings on Vayable or other similar websites.

Go to http://www.vayable.com to sign up.

BUSINESSES COMPLEMENTARY TO RIDESHARING

Carsharing

If you own multiple cars, with one or more sitting idle in your garage or parking stall, you can consider renting them out to tourists, locals, or other rideshare drivers.

GetAround and Turo (formerly RelayRides) are car-sharing services that allow you to list your car for rental in a peer-to-peer market. Popularly, these services have been referred to as the "Airbnb of cars."

GetAround

GetAround is available in San Francisco, Berkeley, Oakland, Chicago, Portland, and Washington, D.C.

GetAround installs an electronic monitoring and security system, including an app-based entry system, making it unnecessary to meet renters in person because they can use the app to pay the rental fee and get into the car.

GetAround fully insures your car against theft and damage. It takes a 40 percent commission on each transaction. Payouts occur monthly.

Visit http://www.getaround.com or your app store for more information. Use my referral code: 10101960759594046 to sign up.

DRIVING PROFITS AND MAKING BANK

HyreCar

HyreCar is a car sharing service that allows you to rent your car out to Uber and Lyft drivers who may not have a car of their own; as such, it's geared for longer-term rentals.

Visit http://hyrecar.com or your app store for more information.

Turo

Turo is available nationwide in cities across forty-nine states (not available in New York) and Ontario, Alberta, and Quebec in Canada.

All renters are vetted through background checks and each rental is insured by Turo for theft and damage. As a loaner, you can set your own prices or let Turo automatically set an "optimal" price based on market conditions in your area and the type of car you have.

For each rental transaction, you and your renters determine pickup or delivery and return arrangements. Since many renters are traveling, it's not uncommon to schedule airport pickups and drop offs.

You keep between 65 and 85 percent of rental fees based

on the level of protection service you purchase from Turo. Fees are paid out within five days.

You can visit http://turo.com or download the app from your app store for more information. Please use my referral code 1409582rDMmlh if you're a new user.

Parking Sharing

The sharing economy even comes down to sharing the private parking stalls in your homes, garages, or driveways, or the parking area in your building.

Know that you can use these apps to share your parking spaces. Know that you can also use them to find cheap or additional parking in your city (or if there are users in your town).

JustPark and Rover Parking are two of the major apps and services in the parking sharing field. The apps allow you to list your parking space, the price of using it (you set the price), and availability. You can also use it to find parking stalls. JustPark will recommend prices depending on the market conditions of your town. Rover allows you to rent at a maximum of $2.00 an hour.

If you're interested in checking out either or both, you can go to the following:

- **JustPark:** Visit justpark.com or download the app from the Apple App Store for iOS or Google Play Store for Android.

- **Rover Parking:** Visit roverparking.com or download the app from the Apple App Store for iOS or the Google Play Store for Android.

Room Sharing

Airbnb has revolutionized the way we travel or find a place to stay when we need short-term accommodations. Many rideshare drivers also dabble in this aspect of the sharing economy, renting spare rooms in their homes to travelers or transplants in need of short-term accommodations. Many bundle their services, providing both a place to stay and a way to get around—selling travelers rideshare transportation or private tour services!

If you have an extra room (or even a couch), consider listing your extra space on Airbnb.

If you're not on Airbnb yet, sign up through my link below and earn rental credits for your first booking.

http://www.airbnb.com/c/jonathanw72

BUSINESSES COMPLEMENTARY TO RIDESHARING

Handywork

Not all of us are interested in driving or sharing our cars or personal space, but some of us may be extremely handy around the house—or good at being personal assistants and completing chores. If this describes you, you can consider hiring yourself out as a handyperson or personal assistant on services like Handy or TaskRabbit. Much like Uber or Lyft, you sign up for the service and sign on and accept jobs through the app as they come in. You could do anything from cleaning someone's home to washing dishes, doing laundry, setting up furniture, hanging something on the wall, snaking a toilet, or picking up the person's meds from the pharmacy.

Handy

Handy connects handy individuals with people who need chores or handiwork done around the home. It is available in thirty cities in the U.S. Examples of jobs include house cleaning, furniture assembly, house painting, electrical work, plumbing work, and other handiwork.

You can download the app from the Apple App Store or Google Play Store of your iOS or Android device.

DRIVING PROFITS AND MAKING BANK

TaskRabbit

TaskRabbit connects handy persons or personal assistants with people who need chores, errands, and handiwork done. It is available in eighteen cities in the U.S.

Visit http://www.taskrabbit.com or download the app from the Apple App Store or Google Play Store of your iOS or Android device for more information.

Dog Walking

If you have a love of animals, you can also take advantage of on-demand dog-walking or dog-sitting opportunities.

Barkly

Barkly is a dog walking service available in Washington, D.C., Philadelphia, and Baltimore.

You can visit http://www.barkly.us to sign up.

Rover

Rover is the largest dog walking and pet sitting on-demand marketplace. It is available in 10,000 cities across the U.S.

You can visit http://www.rover.com to sign up.

Wag!

Wag! is a dog walking and pet sitting service available in the Bay Area, Southern California, New York City, Chicago, Seattle, and Austin.

You can visit http://wagwalking.com to sign up.

Summary

In this chapter, I discussed the multitude of complimentary on-demand and gig-based business opportunities you can leverage in addition to rideshare. Whether you are delivering groceries or takeout food, giving private tours around town, cleaning houses, fixing things around the house, walking dogs, sharing your car or your room, or helping people with errands and chores, there is, literally, no shortage of ways to make money in the on-demand and gig economies.

Driving Forward

Let's diversify your income by checking out some of the other opportunities available in the on-demand, gig, and sharing economies.

- Check out any of the mentioned sites and apps and

decide whether you'd like to pursue any of those opportunities.

- Does doing courier or delivery work interest you?

- Does renting your car, room, or parking space interest you?

- Are you good with your hands or at doing chores? Would work as a TaskRabbit or Handy worker interest you?

- Do you love dogs? Does dog walking or pet sitting for services like Rover, Barkly, or Wag! interest you?

CHAPTER 33

TEN RIDESHARE BUSINESS RECOMMENDATIONS

"When you enjoy what you do, work becomes play."

— Martin Yan

The Rearview Mirror

Throughout this book, I've shared the basics of rideshare driving, the basics of running a business and being self-employed, strategies for boosting your rideshare earnings and developing spin-off businesses, given you a glimpse into the life of a rideshare driver, explained how to handle the less pleasant aspects of driving, and shared additional opportunities to explore that complement rideshare driving. In this final chapter, I will present to you ten recommendations to enhance your chances for success as a rideshare driver as you get ready to get behind the wheel.

1. Be a Good Conversationalist

The core of the rideshare business lies in your professionalism and ability to carry on a conversation. Carrying on a good conversation and having a pleasant personality will help you earn and maintain good ratings. Meeting and getting to know and help other people go about their day is one of the best parts of the job. Carrying on a good conversation will also, ultimately, open up the path to additional opportunities because you'll earn trust, allowing you the opportunity to upsell any additional services you choose to provide.

2. Clean Your Car Daily

Good car hygiene is important! No one wants to ride in a dirty, nasty, stinky car. Practice good hygiene practices on your vehicle to ensure passengers have a pleasant riding experience. Vacuum, sweep, or dust your seats and floors. Wipe down your car's interior. Finally, install a good car freshener scent. These will all have a positive influence on your driver ratings and reviews, keeping you in tip-top shape.

3. Keep Barf Bags in Your Car

This item is especially important when you are driving on weekends or doing the bar closing shift on week nights. If you don't wish to invest in actual barf bags, used plastic shopping bags will suffice. It's good to advise drunk passengers when you pick them up that they are available. I personally keep them shoved into the pouches of the car seats so they are readily visible.

4. Practice Good Car Maintenance Habits

Good car maintenance habits are critical both for your safety and for your passengers' safety, especially since you are on the road more. Things to pay attention to in particular include tire pressure, tire rotation, balance and wheel alignment, oil levels, and checking your other fluid levels and for possible leaks. You should maintain a regular service schedule with your mechanic per your car manual.

5. Print Business Cards

You need to print up business cards. They are one of the best ways to earn return business from passengers or to earn new business when you meet new people. Your business cards should contain the following:

- Your name and contact information—at the very least your phone number

- The range of services you provide (rideshare, private tours, elderly transport, graveyard shift pickups, school pickups or drop offs, grocery runs, bar pickups, etc.)

- Your referrals codes for Uber and Lyft

The best place to source your business cards is Vistaprint. You can use my referral link to get a special deal on your order:

http://vistaprint.extole.com/s/w6w2f

6. Use Professional Accounting Practices

Accurate record keeping and professional advice is critical in helping you to determine how successful your business is and to prepare for tax time. For your accounting purposes, you should either be working with a CPA bookkeeper and tax preparer or be using a professional accounting software program such as QuickBooks.

I personally love QuickBooks for accounting and mileage tracking and for its ability to integrate seamlessly other features such as tax filing and payroll.

Try out QuickBooks Self-Employed with my referral link below with a special deal for new users:

http://fbuy.me/efKwe

7. Retain Professional Legal Advice

As mentioned in Chapter 20, any business person should have access to good legal counsel. As a rideshare driver, you should always be vigilant to avoid traffic violations or car accidents. Your legal counsel can represent you if you are cited or get involved in an accident. Counsel can also assist in dealing with the government should you have problems with your taxes.

In securing legal representation, I personally use and endorse LegalShield, which for a small monthly or annual fee allows me to keep an attorney on retainer 24/7 for both personal and business legal concerns.

You can visit my referral URL below for more information on services, rates, and packages and/or to sign-up.

https://w3.legalshield.com/aasites/Multisite?site=hub&assoc=-jonathankwong

8. Install a Dash Cam

In Chapter 28, I discussed developing a personal safety plan for when you are on the road. Here I reiterate my recommendation to install a dash cam in your vehicle to protect yourself and your passengers. Your footage can serve as valuable evidence should anything happen with a passenger, law enforcement officer, or traffic incident. The Falcon Zero F360 is the most recommended brand and the product I personally use.

9. Develop a Business Mindset

Perhaps the most important thing you can do to develop and grow your rideshare business, and as a business person overall, is to continue to develop and hone your business mindset. It is my hope that this book has ignited a spark in that direction if you have no previous business training or have never considered yourself a business person. Realizing that being a rideshare driver automatically makes you a business person is empowering in and of itself. I encourage you to continue to develop your business mindset and grow as a business person. Keep reading other business books and take business classes, workshops, or seminars as your time and budget allows. Learn and study sales techniques and hone your conversation skills. One of the best business skills you can ever develop is to learn to recognize opportunities when they present themselves and how to capitalize on them. Keep growing as a business person to maximize and achieve your potential.

10. Have Fun!

Perhaps the biggest business and life lesson any of us can learn is simply to have fun in whatever it is we do. Enjoy your adventures as a rideshare driver! Enjoy the people you meet and the sights you get to see. If you're not having fun in what you do, you need to reconsider what it is you are doing.

Summary

In this chapter, I presented ten final tips for you to consider, act on, and remember as you begin your rideshare career. Best wishes moving on and hitting the road as a rideshare driver.

Driving Forward

Take some time to follow up on these ten tips as you begin your career rideshare driving. Be safe out on the road and have fun!

A FINAL WORD

"The power of your dreams lives
in the action—not the vision."

— Robin Sharma

Congratulations on completing *Driving Profits: How to Make Money Ridesharing and Grow Your Business.* Now that you've finished this book, what do you plan to do next? You may have read this book because you have just started your rideshare driving career or you're a current rideshare driver looking to boost your earnings. It is my hope that this book has opened your eyes to possibilities you may not have thought of. I hope this book sparked the business mindset that will serve you throughout the rest of your life. But still, the question remains, "Now what? What do I do next?"

DRIVING PROFITS AND MAKING BANK

I challenge you to take action and start implementing some of the things I discussed in this book. The "Driving Forward" section of each chapter provided you with actionable steps and exercises to help you move forward with your rideshare business. Hopefully, you've completed some of those exercises as we went along. If not, take some time to list out ten actionable steps you can commit to today to move your rideshare business forward.

1. _____
   _____

2. _____
   _____

3. _____
   _____

4. _____
   _____

5. _____
   _____

6. _____
   _____

7. _____
   _____

A FINAL WORD

8. _____
   _____

9. _____
   _____

10. _____
   _____

Over the course of this book, you've learned many things about rideshare driving, small business ownership, and other potential business opportunities you can leverage for yourself in the on-demand, gig, and sharing economies. I also taught you how to recognize and leverage additional business opportunities from your rideshare business. You now have all the tools necessary to operate a successful rideshare business and expand other business opportunities in the future.

I encourage you to contact me at any time in the future. I'd love to know your thoughts on this book, what you liked, what you didn't like, and how I can improve it for future editions. Moreover, I would love to continue to work with you as your small business coach and support team, to help you expand your business and realize your business dreams, so you can lead a fulfilling life. I invite you to schedule a thirty-minute, no-obligation consultation by phone, Skype, Google Hangout, FaceTime, or (if geographically possible) face-to-face to learn how I can assist you more in achieving your dreams!

My email address is jon@akamaivisionary.com and my cell number is (646)-481-5198. Please email or text me with your name and time zone, and I'll be glad to schedule your complimentary consultation.

Wherever you are, I wish you the best and pray for your success in all you do. You deserve all the success and happiness that life brings, and I send out continued prayers for your health, wealth, and happiness.

"In order to succeed, we must first believe that we can."

— Nikos Kazantzakis

To your business and life success!

With aloha, your friend,

Jonathan K Wong

Jonathan Wong, MBA, M.Ed., MPA
Honolulu, Hawaii

APPENDICES

RECOMMENDED APPS

Become a true mobile warrior businessperson and rideshare driver. Download any of the following apps from the Apple App Store or Google Play Store for your iOS or Android device.

Bookkeeping

QuickBooks Self-Employed:

Download here: http://fbuy.me/efKwe

Automate your business bookkeeping. Conveniently connects to your bank, credit card, and PayPal accounts, allowing you to classify income and expenditures as personal or business.

Car Renting

In case you need a loaner car to stay on the road as a driver if your car is in the shop for an extended period, you can try:

HyreCar

Turo: Download here: https://turo.com/refer-ral?code=1409582rDMmlh

DRIVING PROFITS AND MAKING BANK

Countdown

Rideshare Timer: This app helps you count down and track wait times for passengers once you arrive at a destination, so you can cancel with confidence in the event you have a no show.

Emergency Roadside Service

Honk: If you don't have AAA or another roadside assistance program, this app has got your back.

EV Charging

ChargePoint

Greenlots

OpConnect

PlugShare

SemaConnect

If you're driving an electric vehicle, PlugShare helps you find the nearest charging stations and their occupancy. The other apps represent the major charging providers in the nation. Accounts on their apps allow you easy access and payment for the chargers in their networks.

Flight Tracking

Flightstats: Track flight arrival times so you can be at the airport in the waiting area and get airport fares.

Gas Pricing

Gas Buddy: Find the nearest, cheapest gas station.

Mileage Tracking

Hurdlr

MileIQ

QuickBooks Self-Employed: http://fbuy.me/efKwe

SherpaShare

Use any of these apps to keep track of your business mileage with simple swipes to classify and distinguish between personal rides and business rides.

DRIVING PROFITS AND MAKING BANK

Mobile Credit Card Processing

Intuit GoPay

PayPal Here

Square

Use these to process rider tips or make in car sales of refreshments, private tours or other products and services you sell to passengers.

Parking Spaces

Rover

JustPark

In case you need a break and want to find cheap parking in the area.

Weather Tracking

AccuWeather: When the weather gets bad, Surges and Prime-time fares go up. Track the weather and know when to be on the road for the best fares.

APPENDIX B

RESOURCE LIST

Accounting, Bookkeeping, and Tax Preparation

QuickBooks Self-Employed

http://fbuy.me/efKwe

Hands down, the industry leader for business accounting apps. It helps you keep track of revenues and expenses, provides tax optimization suggestions, and tracks your business mileage.

Business Cards and Brochures

Vistaprint

http://vistaprint.extole.com/s/w6w2f

The industry leader in on-demand business graphics, collateral materials, and printing.

Legal Services

LegalShield

https://w3.legalshield.com/aasites/Multisite?site=hub&assoc=-jonathankwong

Get affordable legal assistance 24/7 with an attorney on speed dial. Individual, family, and business plans are available starting at $200/yr to $500/yr. Get assistance with anything from traffic citations, representation in the event of car accidents, or IRS audit protection plus WAY MORE.

Rideshare Online Communities and Blogs

The Rideshare Guy

http://therideshareguy.com/

Easily the best blog in the world on Rideshare.

ABOUT THE AUTHOR

Jonathan K. Wong, MBA, M.Ed., MPA is a Honolulu-born and based author, blogger, podcaster, professional speaker, success coach, and organizational consultant. A former college instructor, counselor, technology trainer, instructional designer, and administrative professional of fifteen years alongside being a trained and certified Information Technology professional, Jonathan now travels the road teaching success seminars and workshops and delivering keynotes on topics such as academic success and career, business, and leadership development. A Native-Hawaiian professional, he takes special interest in working with indigenous and minority-serving clients and organizations.

Throughout his academic career, Jonathan earned his advanced degrees in business administration, education technology, and public administration, and over the years, he has lent his expertise in technology and business to various individuals and organizations through his Akamai Visionary Consulting practice.

Jonathan's hobbies include studying the martial arts; learning about alternative, traditional, and complementary healing styles; playing video games; and watching superhero movies and professional wrestling. He has extensive studies in Chinese kung fu in the Hung Gar and Choy Li Fut styles, Okinawan Karate in the Shorin-Ryu and Uechi Ryu styles, Muay Thai boxing, Brazilian Jiu-Jitsu, and the ancient Hawaiian martial art of Lua. In his alternative and complementary healing studies, he has done extensive study as an energy healer and bodyworker, having certified as a Reiki Master (Usui style) and Pranic Healer, and has studied bodywork modalities, including Thai Massage, Reflexology, Cranial Sacral Therapy, and Hawaiian Lomilomi.

A part-time performance artist, Jonathan is trained in improvisational theatre and as a TV, film, and voice actor. He performed for several years with several Honolulu-based troupes and theatre companies in short form and long form improv. As an actor, he occasionally performs supporting roles in various independent films and web productions, and he provides voice work for various projects.

He is always available for success coaching, organizational consulting, trainings, seminars, workshops, and keynote speaking gigs.

Jonathan resides in Honolulu with his fiancée Liane.

AKAMAI
VISIONARY CONSULTING

Start Your Small Business Today!

Akamai Visionary Consulting is the small business consulting and coaching practice Jonathan Wong runs to help the everyday person start and grow a small business. If you're interested in learning more about ridesharing business opportunities or have other small business dreams, Jonathan will be glad to work with you.

As a trained MBA and certified IT professional, Jonathan offers his deep knowledge of both business and technology to help individuals develop sound businesses. Jonathan is glad to assist you in developing your business plan, business strategic plan, and marketing plans as well as providing you with various technology solutions to help automate your marketing. In growing your business, he will assist you in developing the business savvy and leadership skills you need to thrive. Whether you wish to develop your business, start your business, optimize your business, or expand your business, Jonathan and Akamai Visionary Consulting can provide what you need.

Visit akamaivisionary.com or call or text (646) 481-5198 or email jon@akamaivisionary.com for consultation rates and packages.

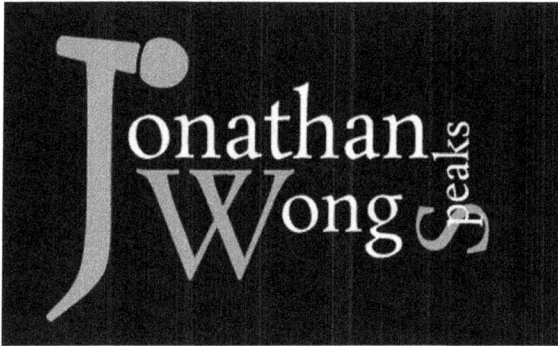

Jonathan Speaks

Entertain * Educate * Engage

As a gifted and prolific speaker and entertainer, Jonathan Wong draws on his years of studies, teaching experience, and performance background to craft a unique presentation for your audience.

An instructor and trainer of fifteen years with expertise in leadership, academic success skills, business, health and wellness, life balance, and goal setting, Jonathan speaks on various topics of interest to business associations, corporations, and governments.

A performing artist of over a decade, Jonathan is a trained actor, comedian, and musician, having performed on Honolulu's improv, sketch, stand-up comedy, and independent film scene for over ten years. Raised in a musical family and having gone on to elective music studies at the high school and college level, today Jonathan is a vocalist, guitarist, and ukulele musician who covers genres ranging from inspirational music to acoustic contemporary. His speaking engagements always hit the mark in terms of educating the audience on the topic while providing an entertaining and engaging experience that incorporates a unique combination of comedic and musical entertainment.

Hire Jonathan today for any of the following:

- Conference keynotes
- Association keynotes
- Corporate trainings
- Government trainings

Speaking Topics Include:

- Starting-Up for Success
- Developing Your Inner Leader
- Developing a High Performance Championship Team
- The Superstar Solopreneur
- Building a Hall of Fame Career
- Leading a Balanced Life When It All Needs to Be Done

- Overcoming Depression and Other Mental Illnesses
- Bouncing Back from Failures and Setbacks
- Running a Lean Organization

To discuss with Jonathan how he can wow your audience and leave it wanting more, contact him at:

http://www.jonathanwongspeaks.com
Phone/Text: (213) 262-9570
Email: jonathanwong.bookings@gmail.com

DRIVING PROFITS: THE COURSE

Expand your knowledge on the rideshare business and business in general beyond what was covered in this book. Boost your learning by enrolling in the "Driving Profits Course," available at: http://www.drivingprofitsandmakingbank.com

As a course member, you'll have lifetime access to course content and lifetime access to the growing community of students and drivers.

TALES FROM BEHIND THE WHEEL: YEAR ONE

Want to know more about the life of a rideshare driver? Get your copy of *Tales from Behind the Wheel: Year One*. For your pleasure and entertainment, Jonathan Wong shares more than fifty true life stories from his first year as a driver. From hilarious moments to downright OMG, WTF, wow moments, he takes you behind the wheel as he reflects on memorable moments from his first year as a driver.

Tales from Behind the Wheel: Year One is available at:

www.TalesFromBehindTheWheel.com
Amazon, iBooks, Google Play Books, and Audible.

LEGALSHIELD

Get an Affordable Attorney When You Need One

Get a law firm on speed dial!

You never know when you could use an attorney's assistance.

LegalShield members rest confidently, knowing if a legal matter arises, they are represented and covered with competent legal help. LegalShield members enjoy the following benefits:

- Legal advice and counsel
- Letters and phone calls made on your behalf
- Legal document review
- Preparation of Wills and Medical Powers of Attorney
- Traffic citation defense
- Trial defense, including pretrial and trial time (not available in all states)
- Divorce and separation services
- Adoption services
- 24/7 Emergency Response and Availability
- IRS audit representation

Individual Plans start at $17.95/month in most states, $19.95/month for Family Plans. Business Plans start at an additional $9.95/month. Supplemental trial defense (additional hours) coverage is available for an additional $9.95/month. Identity Theft protection plans start at $9.95/month. For more information visit:

https://w3.legalshield.com/aasites/
Multisite?site=hub&assoc=jonathankwong

SUCCEEDING IN COLLEGE AND LIFE

Jonathan Wong's first book, *Succeeding in College and Life,* is geared toward college students or college-bound high school students with the goal of equipping them for success in the college classroom and beyond.

A college instructor and counselor of fifteen years, Jonathan provides all the information any prospective or current college student needs to excel in school and far beyond.

Succeeding in College and Life covers in-depth many topics of interest to students, including how to study and manage your time; how to balance extracurricular activities, your finances, new relationships, possible homesickness; and how to make the best choices that will give you an advantage when you enter the job market.

- Students will discover how to:
- Pick the right school for you
- Pick the right major and career field

- Fund your education so you can stay in school

- Practice effective study skills, including notetaking, brain-storming, and skimming

- Manage your time so you can get more done

- Earn and manage money

- Take advantage of technology to make your studies near effortless

- Build relationships and networks to succeed in school and launch your career

Whether you're a current or prospective college student, *Succeeding in College and Life* is your one-stop source for all the information you need to succeed in your studies. When you leverage the skills you will learn here, you'll be able to create the life you deserve for yourself and the ones you love.

Buy your copy today at succeedingincollegeandlife.com, Amazon, iBooks, Google Play, or Audible.